THAT THEIR SOULS MAY BE SAVED

...OF CHURCH DISCIPLINE

Durhams
Monday, 3/30
6:30 p.m.
✓
RSVP 314-5617

Peaceful House Publishing
3617 N. Georgetown Drive
Montgomery, Alabama

Copyright 2008

ISBN: 978-0-9762140-3-8

Printed in China

Layout and Design Rob Baker

All rights reserved. No part of this book may be reproduced in any form without permission from the publisher, except in the case of brief quotations embodied in articles or critical reviews.

Contents

Forward iii

1. Trouble in Tulsa 1
2. The Command to Discipline 15
3. A Little Leaven Leavens The Whole Lump 25
4. Judge Righteous Judgment 37
5. In The Name of Jesus Christ 47
6. The Fatal Flaw of Non-discipline 57
7. It Just Won't Work 69
8. We Are Not Detectives 83
9. This Is Going To Hurt 95
10. When The Wayward Return 107
11. The Proper Procedure For Disfellowship 117
12. What Sins Would Call For Withdrawal? 129
13. A Biblical Test Case 143

Appendix A — Self Withdrawal 151

Appendix B — An Actual Letter 159

Dedication

To the faithful elders, deacons, and saints of the Ironaton church of Christ, who have supported me faithfully in my efforts in the Lord's Kingdom and who hold fast to the biblical command to lovingly administer church discipline.

Special thanks to all those who added helpful information and insight to make this book more effective, especially to Jason Hilburn who helped procure the letter that composes Appendix B.

Forward

The Church of our Lord is my home. From my very birth, I have been reared in a family that loves and appreciates the church of Christ. My father is a Gospel preacher, and has been for almost 30 years. My oldest brother has been preaching full-time for about seven years, my middle brother is currently a youth minister, my mother travels to various congregations teaching ladies' classes and teenage girls at camps in the Summers. I have been preaching and writing for about 10 years. All of our wives and children are active in the work of the Church. The Lord's Church is my life. The heroes of my youth were the Gospel preachers who would gather around our dinner table, tell jokes, and stay up late with my parents talking "Jesus" and "the Church" for hours after we three boys had gone to bed. I love the Church, think of her often and fondly, and enjoy nothing more than sitting around with my wife and members of the Church discussing "church" stuff like VBS, potlucks, Bible class, and bringing the lost to Christ.

I say all that to say that I bear absolutely no ill-will toward the Church. I have no axe to grind. No malice or envy of any sort motivates the writing of this book on church discipline and disfellowship. My sole reason for writing this book is because, in my experiences in the Church, disfellowship is one of, if not the, most neglected commands by congregations of the Lord's Church that are otherwise very solid and obedient. It is high time that we as the members of the church of Christ revisit the command to disfellowship, repent of our neglect, and move forward in our obedience to God's command to withdraw from those who walk disorderly (2 Thessalonians 3:6), so that their souls may be saved in the day of our Lord Jesus (1 Corinthians 5:5).

Chapter 1
Trouble In Tulsa

In the final analysis, the Lord used this situation to bring glory to His name, His Church, and the faithful brethren who stood strong in their obedience to His command.

Chapter 1

> "For the eyes of the Lord run to and fro throughout the whole earth, to show Himself strong on behalf of those whose heart is loyal to Him."
> (2 Chronicles 16:9)

Rarely does news about the Lord's church reach major media outlets such as national television or *Time Magazine*. This particular episode in the life of the Lord's church, however, happened to make headline news. The March 26, 1984, *Time Magazine* article bears the innocent sounding title "Marian and the Elders." The article proceeds to summarize a court case in which a member of the church of Christ named Marian Guinn sued her eldership for 1.3 million dollars for alleged damages she received from being disfellowshiped. She was granted $390,000 in the initial ruling that took place in 1984 in Tulsa, Oklahoma.

As the *Time Magazine* article and other court documents record, Marian attended the Collinsville church of Christ, in Collinsville, Oklahoma. She was divorced and had three children when she associated herself with the brethren there.

A few years later, she engaged in an ongoing sexual relationship with a man in Collinsville. She confessed this sinful relationship to the elders but refused to repent of her sin and remove herself from the situation. On three different occasions, the elders confronted her about the sinful lifestyle she was living. She refused to repent. During the third and final confrontation, the elders informed Marian that they would publicly notify the congregation and withdraw fellowship from her if she refused to confess her sin to the congregation and repent.

On September 25, 1981, soon after the elders informed her of their decision, Marian wrote them a letter asking them not to publicly disfellowship her, but instead to tell the congregation she had withdrawn her membership. The elders refused her request and, on October 4, read to the congregation the Scriptures that Marian had violated and publicly disfellowshiped her. She then sued the congregation and was granted $390,000.

As is often the case, this "juicy" news spread to the media and caused quite a stir. Popular talk show host, Phil Donahue, picked up the story and invited Marian and her lawyer to appear on his show, along with a representative sampling of various members of the church of Christ. Garland Elkins, of the Memphis School of preaching, also appeared on the show as an "unofficial" spokesman for churches of Christ. The showdown was interesting, to say the least. Phil Donahue would ask Garland Elkins a question, to which Garland Elkins would respond primarily with a verbatim quote from the Scriptures. Questions continued to come from the audience and Donahue, most of which were met with verbatim quotes from Scripture. Finally, one woman in the audience was given the floor and she said in so many words, "I know what you people's problem is, you are blinded by the Bible." Needless to say, the Scriptural authority and commendation of the Collinsville elders' actions was lost on the national audience as a whole.

> "I know what you people's problem is, you are blinded by the Bible."

That court case was tried over twenty years ago, but the devastating memory of it has haunted elders' meetings and discussions of disfellowship for the entirety of those two decades. How often has some faithful brother broached the topic of church discipline in an elders' meeting or a men's meeting, only to hear his suggestion shot down with a statement like, "You remember what happened in Collinsville." How many times have church leaders in this country for the last twenty years continued to allow sinful men and women to sit, undisciplined and unchecked, in their assemblies because the leaders were afraid that any action on their part might land them in a lengthy, costly court battle? "Remember Collinsville," has become the battle cry, or more appropriately, the call to retreat, whispered into the ear of conscientious brethren throughout the United States. And sadly, Satan has accomplished his desired effect, with thousands of congregations of the Lord's church scared to death to take any action to disfellowship the wayward for fear of legal action and monetary loss.

Brethren, it is long past time that we laid bare this business of avoiding God-ordained action based on the idea that it might cost us something. If we can show that disfellowship is commanded by God, then we as the body of Christ must be ready and willing to obey God's command, come what may. Can you imagine Peter and John considering whether or not they were going to lose money or be sued if they preached the Gospel of Christ? Indeed not. When confronted by the leaders of the Jews, who had warned them not to preach Jesus, "Peter and the other apostles answered and said, 'We ought to obey God rather than men'" (Acts 5:28-29). It is time we realize that to avoid church discipline because we might get sued or lose money is simply cowardice and unfaithfulness. Do we no longer believe that God's hand works in the affairs of men in such a way as to glorify His name and vindicate the righteous?

And what if we lose every building we own and every penny in our treasuries because we are standing for the Truth? Others have sacrificed far more than this. The Bible reminds us that the Lord's people were "stoned, they were sawn in two, were tempted, were slain with the sword. They wandered about in sheepskins and goatskins, being destitute, afflicted, tormented—of whom the world was not worthy. They wandered in deserts and mountains, in dens and caves of the earth" (Hebrews 10: 37-38). What would one of those

That Their Souls Might Be Saved

faithful brethren who had been sawn in two think about a person or group of people who would not obey a God-given command because it might mean that some legal action may follow and some money might be lost? More importantly, what would God think? Neglecting to properly discipline wayward members is to deny the authority of the Word of God and to willfully disobey it. As James wrote: "Therefore, to him who knows to do good and does not do it, to him it is sin" (4:17). The Hebrews writer stated it even more emphatically when he wrote: "For if we sin willfully after we have received the knowledge of the truth, there no longer remains a sacrifice for sins, but a certain fearful expectation of the judgment" (Hebrews 10:26-27).

THE REST OF THE STORY

Furthermore, it is high time that those in the Lord's church were given the opportunity to hear, as the well-known radio personality Paul Harvey so quaintly puts it, the rest of the story. Marian Guinn and her case against the elders at Collinsville did not end with her receiving $390,000. Instead, the case was appealed until it eventually landed on the docket of the Oklahoma Supreme Court. In the appeal, the highest court in the state reversed the judgment and remanded the case to be tried again. The case was then settled out of court.

More interesting than the reversal of judgment are some of the statements found in the official court documents. Under the section titled "Facts," paragraph 3, the documents read: "The Church of Christ follows a literal interpretation of the Bible which serves as the church's sole source of moral, religious and ethical guidance. When confronted with the allegation, Parishioner [Marian Guinn– KB] admitted violating the Church of Christ's prohibition against fornication. As a transgressor of the denomination's code of ethics, Parishioner became subject to the disciplinary procedure set forth in Matthew 18:13-17" (Guinn v. Church of Christ Collinsville).

> "Therefore, to him who knows to do good and does not do it, to him it is sin."

We need to notice several significant things concerning this telling statement. First, the highest court in the state of Oklahoma admitted and recognized that the church of Christ has no man-made creed book, no humanly concocted statement of faith, and no other source of guidance than the Bible. Second, although the court improperly designated the church as a denomination, it rightly determined that the guilty member of the church should be disciplined according to Matthew 18:13-17.

> "This serves the purpose of purification of the Church and to prevent the sin from spreading."

In conjunction with this, the next paragraph in the "Facts" of the case states: "The Elders carried out the **biblically-mandated** disciplinary procedure in three stages, with the entire process lasting more than a year" (emphasis added). Is it not ironic that the highest secular court in the state of Oklahoma recognized the obvious fact that church discipline is a biblically-mandated procedure? And yet, many congregations of the Lord's church have failed to acknowledge this fact, or at least have failed to act upon it.

Other comments in the court documents are equally as impressive. Under a section titled "Post-Withdrawal Actions," the following statement is made: "Because the Church believes members of all churches which practice the precepts of the New Testament of the Bible constitute the universal Church, their disciplinary procedures include notification of nearby churches of Parishioner's withdrawal of fellowship. This serves the purpose of purification of the Church and to prevent the sin from spreading." How amazingly accurate the Oklahoma Supreme Court was in its assessment of many of the major beliefs of the Lord's Church, including the fact that every congregation which practices the precepts in the New Testament belongs to the universal church of Jesus Christ!

Conclusion

What really happened in Tulsa? After seeing the rest of the story, God's providential work in this episode is unmistakable. An eldership that faithfully followed the biblical command to disfellowship a sinful sister was persecuted for their obedience to God. Because of this incident, a faithful, knowledgable brother was invited to present the biblical case for discipline on a national television show, which he did quite effectively. Those watching the show may have failed to appreciate the Lord's Word on the subject, but they could not deny that the church in this case was being faithful to God's commands as contained in the Bible.

After approximately five years, when the case was finally appealed to the highest court in the state of Oklahoma, the official court documents have recorded for all posterity several powerful and accurate statements detailing some of the most basic tenets of the church of Christ, not the least of which is the fact that the church has no other source of moral, ethical, or religious guidance than the Bible. The court also concurred that the elders were following a "biblically-mandated" procedure. In the final analysis, the Lord used this situation to bring glory to His name, His church, and the faithful brethren who stood strong in their obedience to His command to withdraw from the sinful sister who was walking disorderly. Oh, that we truly would "Remember Collinsville" and let that memory spur us on to faithfully follow the biblically-mandated disciplinary procedures in our churches.

[Official documents of the case can be procured from http://wyomcases.courts.state.wy.us/applications/oscn/DeliverDocument.asp?citeID=10494; Also, the *Time Magazine* article can be accessed at http://www.time.com/time/archive/printout/0,23657,921655,00.html.]

Chapter 1

Discussion Questions

1. What things did the Oklahoma Supreme Court understand about the church of Christ that many of our own members seem not to grasp?

2. List and discuss some of the primary reasons why church discipline is not practiced as it should be in many congregations.

3. Why do you think news about the Lord's church rarely reaches the national media? When such news has reached the media, what type of image does the media portray of the church? Why do you think the Lord allowed this particular story to hit the news?

4. What biblical point does the response from the audience on the Donahue program make? Consider verses like Matthew 13:14-19 in your answer.

5. What types of attitudes would cause a person to take the legal actions Marian Guinn took? How can such attitudes be avoided? What types of attitudes should Marian have shown in response to the elder's actions?

CHAPTER 2

The Command To Discipline

One explicit command of God seems to have been left off the "check-list" of many otherwise obedient and faithful congregations—the command to withdraw from wayward members.

Chapter 2

> "But we command you, brethren, in the name of our Lord Jesus Christ, that you withdraw from every brother who walks disorderly and not according to the tradition which he received from us."
> (2 Thessalonians 3:6)

Many things in the Lord's church are optional. Whether or not a congregation decides to meet on Wednesday night, Tuesday night, or any other night of the week is completely optional. When the Lord's Supper is eaten, whether it is done before the sermon or after the sermon, is a matter of opinion, as long as it is done on the first day of the week. No biblical command tells congregations how many songs to sing on Sunday morning or how many prayers to lead at any given service. God, in His infinite wisdom, has seen fit to leave some things to the discretion of the individual congregation and the judgment of the elders.

Other things, however, are not optional. In some matters, God has given specific commands as to what He does or does not want done. It is a command for a congregation to gather together to eat the Lord's Supper and remember Christ's death (1 Corinthians 11:23-26). It is a command for the members of the church of Christ to worship by singing and making melody in their hearts to God (Ephesians 5:19). It is a command for the Lord's church to have only male preachers in the pulpits (1 Timothy 2:12). Such commands are to be followed without question and without compromise. A faithful congregation of the Lord's church will be following all such commands in a spirit of humble obedience. Such a humble, obedient spirit thrives and is manifestly evident in numerous congregations all across the United States and the rest of the world.

However one explicit command of God seems to have been left off the "check-list" of many otherwise obedient and faithful congregations—the command to withdraw from wayward members. Ironically, the statements that command such withdrawal are more explicit and unambiguous than many other commands that are faithfully followed. For instance, Paul penned these words to the church at Thessalonica: "But we command you, brethren, in the name of our Lord Jesus Christ, that you withdraw from every brother who walks disorderly and not according to the tradition which he received from us.... And if anyone does not obey our word in this epistle, note that person, and do not keep company with him, that he may be ashamed" (2 Thessalonians 3:6, 14). One would be hard pressed to find in the Scriptures a more direct statement than Paul's "we command you" in verse six. Obviously, God wanted this command to be crystal clear, unambiguous, and shrouded in no uncertain terms. A direct command was issued to the Thessalonians and to all congregations of the Lord's church to withdraw fellowship from those who walk disorderly. (In a later chapter we will define more specifically what "walking disorderly" entails. At this juncture, it is important not to miss the simple fact that there is a very clear command to withdraw.) In 1 Corinthians 5, Paul gives very specific instructions regarding withdrawal from a wayward member, explaining to the brethren that they were "not to keep company with anyone named a brother, who is a fornicator, or covetous, or an idolater, or a reviler, or a drunkard, or an extortioner—not even to eat with such a person....

> **God wanted this command to be crystal clear, unambiguous, and shrouded in no uncertain terms.**

Therefore 'put away from yourselves that wicked person'" (vss. 11, 13). One cannot read through the New Testament and miss the fact that congregations are under a direct command from God to withdraw from wayward members.

It is wonderful that a person can attend any number of biblically sound congregations of the Lord's church on any given Sunday and join with that congregation in scriptural singing in worship to God. It is equally as laudable that a person can go into those same congregations and partake of the Lord's Supper, consisting of the same elements that were used almost 2,000 years ago, when the Lord Himself instituted that glorious memorial feast. In those same congregations, it is refreshing to know that a person can sit in the pew and hear God's plan for the salvation of man's soul delivered from the pulpit, unchanged and just as powerful as it was when it was originally preached by the apostles themselves. But it is the sad truth that an individual could have been in the pews of many of those same congregations every Sunday for the past 5, 10, or 20 years and have never seen a person publicly disciplined. It would be wonderful to imagine that such is the situation because there have been no wayward members, but that is simply not the case. Many of those congregations that have been so faithful in other areas have chosen, especially in the past 20 years, to neglect the command to withdraw fellowship. The majority of you reading this know that such is the case. You are the ones who have been sitting in those pews for the past 10-20 years bearing silent witness to this fact. Many of you saw public withdrawal done in the days of your parents or in "years gone by," but you are acutely aware of its absence in recent years.

Numerous reasons for this tragic neglect could be suggested. It could be that there has been a lack of persistent, biblical teaching on the subject. Because of this lack of teaching, some members who have not done much personal Bible study simply may not be aware of the command to withdraw. In such cases, solid, consistent, and biblical teaching should help remedy the problem. It could also be the case that congregations are aware of the teaching, but have looked to sister congregations to see if they are following the command. If they notice that surrounding congregations are not practicing church discipline, they may have decided that it is not something for them either. They may have fallen prey to "measuring themselves by themselves, and comparing themselves among themselves." Paul considered such individuals and congregations "unwise" (2 Corinthians 10:12). It may also be the case that the negative influence of the greater religious world has infiltrated the Lord's church. We live in a society that abhors anything that seems judgmental, intolerant, or harsh. Our society accepts almost everything and everyone, except those who denounce another's actions as sinful and wrong. Such a spirit of misguided tolerance may be a factor in the church's neglect to disfellowship the wayward.

Whatever the reasons may be, we must not let them persist any longer. We must repent of our negligence and be committed in humble obedience to the command to practice church discipline. If we continue to follow many of God's commands, and yet persist in our slackness to withdraw, we are "guilty of all." James summarized the situation well when he wrote: "For whoever shall keep the whole

> **We must repent of our negligence and be committed in humble obedience to the command to practice church discipline.**

law, and yet stumble in one point, he is guilty of all. For He who said, 'Do not commit adultery,' also said, 'Do not murder.' Now if you do not commit adultery, but you do murder, you have become a transgressor of the law" (James 2:10-11). We all understand that if a congregation were obeying God in every other point but persisting in having a woman preacher or elder, then that congregation would not be faithfully following God's Word. We understand equally as well that if a congregation were obedient to every other command but taught that individuals did not need to be baptized to come in contact with Christ's blood, then such a congregation would be unfaithful. Is it not equally true, then, to state that a congregation that faithfully follows all other commands but continues to neglect to disfellowship wayward members falls under the same condemnation as those who err in relation to baptism or women's role?

Let us eagerly listen to the admonition of the Hebrews writer, and "give the more earnest heed to the things we have heard, lest we drift away" (Hebrews 2:1).

CHAPTER 2
DISCUSSION QUESTIONS

1. How do biblical statements regarding church discipline compare to statements regarding other things done by the church such as eating the Lord's Supper or singing without instruments?

2. Why do you think many other commandments in the Bible are obeyed, but the command to publicly discipline is often neglected? What factors in our society would lead to this type of neglect?

3. Discuss the nature of acceptable obedience to God. Why must humans obey God? What types of reactions are not acceptable responses to a command from God?

4. Discuss why neglecting a single command, while obeying the others, places a person or congregation in a disobedient state. Give some examples of religious groups guilty of this. Factor verses like James 2:1-13, Ecclesiastes 10:1, and Mark 10:17-22 into your answer.

5. What areas of your personal life need to be evaluated or altered so that you are not allowing a single vice to disrupt your relationship with God? What steps are you willing to take to make changes in this area?

Chapter 3

A Little Leaven Leavens The Whole Lump

The biblical record is replete with statements and narratives that demonstrate the infectious, pervasive nature of sin.

Chapter 3

> "Your glorying is not good. Do you not know that a little leaven leavens the whole lump."
> (1 Corinthians 5:6)

Any person who has ever baked yeast rolls or sour dough bread understands the principle of leavening. Leaven is the key ingredient that causes bread to "rise" into a beautiful loaf or delicious yeast roll. One small packet of yeast or a single cup of sour dough "starter" can provide enough rising power to motivate several loaves of bread into perfect shapeliness. That is the nature of yeast or leaven; it does not take much to influence the entire loaf. Another aspect of leaven or yeast is the fact that it causes bread to rise due to a decaying process. As the substance decays, it releases gasses that bubble into the surrounding dough and cause it to expand. This decaying process gives the bread a slightly sour taste.

In 1 Corinthians 5:6 Paul made a spiritual application to the physical properties of leaven. He asked the Corinthians an obviously rhetorical question: "Do you not know that a little leaven leavens the whole lump?"

The answer to Paul's rhetorical question was abundantly clear. Of course the Corinthians knew that a little leaven would influence an entire loaf. What they failed to realize, however, was that the spiritual decay that they were allowing to persist in their congregation would eventually encourage widespread spiritual decomposition throughout the entire congregation. If left unchecked, it could then spread through other congregations and eventually the entire body of Christ could become infected with the unrestrained sin in Corinth. One of the primary reasons that congregations are commanded to withdraw fellowship from wayward brethren is because undisciplined sin is contagious.

> **Undisciplined sin is contagious.**

The biblical record is replete with statements and narratives that demonstrate the infectious, pervasive nature of sin, and God's insistence that action be taken to curtail the spread of it. For example, the failure of the Israelites to enter into the Promised Land stands as one of the most tragic examples of sin's infectious nature. The twelve spies sent to search out the land brought back a glowing report of a lush, verdant paradise flowing with milk and honey. Yet, the ten spies' refusal to recognize the power of God caused them to bemoan the fact that the inhabitants of Canaan were too strong, and their cities too well fortified to be conquered. In spite of the passionate and reasonable protests of Joshua, Caleb, Moses, and Aaron, the negative influence of those ten men caused an entire nation of approximately six hundred thousand fighting men (not counting women and children) to wander in the deserted wilderness for forty arduous years. Every one who was twenty or older at the time (besides Joshua and Caleb) died during the wilderness wandering, and the ten wicked spies died of a plague before the Lord. In a few brief moments, the infectious negativism of sin had spread throughout the camp of Israel and caused massive destruction (Numbers 14). Such is the nature of sin. It is like kudzu in the south, it spreads relentlessly if left unchecked for even the briefest period of time.

The familiar story of Nadab and Abihu provides another compelling Old Testament example of the fact that sin has contagious potential. These two young men were given a place of prominence and respect in the worship of God. But they chose to neglect God's commands and offer profane fire in their service to Him. In response to this sinful action "fire went out from the Lord and devoured them, and they died before the Lord" (Leviticus 10:2). In Moses' reply to Aaron justifying God's action, he stated that the action was appropriate based on God's statement: "By those who come near Me I must be regarded as holy; and before all the people I must be glorified" (10:3). Since Nadab and Abihu had profaned God's name and disobeyed His command in the sight of all the people, they had to be dealt with quickly, strictly, and in a public manner so that the entire congregation would understand the seriousness of sin and its consequences.

This principle of public discipline for the purpose of preventing the spread of sin can be seen even more clearly in Deuteronomy 13:6-11. In these verses, Moses explained to the Israelites that anyone who tempted them to worship other gods should be put to death. He specifically mentioned the fact that even though the tempter might be a wife, a brother, a son, a daughter, or a friend, no mercy should be shown to the idolatrous rebel. In fact, whoever was tempted by this individual should be the first one to put his or her "hand against him to put him to death, and afterward the hand of all the people" (13:9). Moses further instructed the Israelites concerning such a one: "And you shall stone him with stones until he dies, because he sought to entice you away from the Lord your God…" (13:10). What justification did Moses provide to account for such stringent measures regarding the insidious idolater? He stated that these actions were necessary, "So all Israel shall hear and fear, and not again do such wickedness as this among you" (13:11). In almost identical language, any person who would not obey the orders of the priest was to be put to death so that "all the people shall hear and fear, and no longer act presumptuously" (17:13).

The punishment of the tempter or rebellious person was not only designed to appropriate to the individual the righteous judgment due to him, but in a larger context, such public punishment was to provide a restraining effect upon the entire congregation. When correctly administered, public punishment and discipline were vital to the overall faithfulness of the entire nation.

New Testament examples of this principle abound as well. Among the most familiar is the memorable story of Ananias and his wife Sapphira (Acts 5:1-11). During a time of financial difficulty for the New Testament church, many Christians "who were possessors of lands or houses sold them, and brought the proceeds of the things that were sold, and laid them at the apostles' feet" (Acts 4:34-35). Apparently, Ananias and Sapphira had a piece of property that they sold for the purpose of giving the proceeds to the Lord. When they sold the land, however, they decided to keep back a portion of the profit and lie to the apostles about the money they had received. They wanted to appear "righteous" by presenting the false idea that they were giving the total amount of money they received. Of course, they neglected to calculate into their conspiratorial plans that lying to God would carry with it serious consequences. When Ananias lied about the transaction, he immediately "fell down and breathed his last" (Acts 5:5). About three hours later, his wife arrived on the scene, was questioned by Peter, and lied in a similar manner. She too "fell down…and breathed her last" (5:10). What effect did the death of this couple have on the church as a whole? Verse 11 of chapter 5 states: "So great fear came upon all the church and upon all who heard these things." God knew that such a public display of punishment would be an extremely effective deterrent to those who might have been tempted to sin in a similar fashion. Once again, it is obvious that public punishment and correction not only administered justice to the individuals deserving the treatment, but such actions also prevented similar sins among the church as a whole.

> **Those who are sinning rebuke in the presence of all that the rest also may fear.**

In his instructions to Timothy, Paul reiterated this very idea. Paul detailed the procedures to be followed in receiving an accusation against an elder. He wrote: "Those who are sinning rebuke in the presence of all" (1 Timothy 5:20). He immediately followed this statement with the reason for such public denunciation, "that the rest also may fear."

Sadly, numerous congregations throughout the brotherhood today provide painful reminders of the consequences of a lack of public discipline. Often it is the case that a couple in a congregation will be living in an adulterous situation as it relates to marriage, divorce, and remarriage. Because of their "sweet" dispositions and their pleasant personalities, they will be allowed to worship with the congregation, and even lead in different ways. Others in the congregation witness the neglected discipline, and all too often the congregation begins to attract those in similar sinful situations. In time, the congregation becomes a "haven" for those in adulterous unions, and the failure to disfellowship the original couple has caused widespread spiritual decay to "leaven" the entire congregation–for generations to come.

Conclusion

From the biblical statements and examples discussed, it cannot be denied that public denunciation of sin is necessary, not only for the good of the individual being disciplined, but also for the good of the church as a whole. Since it is true that "a little leaven leavens the whole lump," congregations must be diligent to "purge out the old leaven" that they may be "a new lump" not tainted by the infectious nature of unchecked sin (1 Corinthians 5:7).

Chapter 3

Discussion questions

1. From reading this chapter, explain one of the primary purposes for church discipline. Give Bible verses that support your answers.

2. In the illustrations given in the chapter, what effect does the public denunciation of sin often have? Does it always have this effect? Consider factors that would hinder this response.

3. Discuss biblical illustrations not listed in the chapter in which sin was not dealt with and it spread to others. Do the same with sins in our modern society.

4. It is the case that an individual's sin often affects many people besides the sinner. How does the idea that "no man is an island" relate to this discussion? Consider some examples in which one person's sin dramatically impacts those around him/her.

5. While it is true that unchecked sin often spreads, it is also true that a few righteous people or actions can motivate others to do good works. List some biblical examples of this. Consider New Testament verses such as Hebrews 11:24-25 in your discussion.

Chapter 4

Judge Righteous Judgment

What, then, would classify as "righteous judgment"? How is one to determine what type of judgment is righteous and what type is unrighteous?

Chapter 4

> "Do not judge according to appearance, but judge with righteous judgment."
> (John 7:24)

It is readily apparent that many worldly people who live sinful lifestyles have little time for the teachings of Jesus found in the New Testament. They do, however, seem to have one verse well committed to memory—Matthew 7:1. The scenario goes something like this. A Christian makes a statement that a certain kind of lifestyle is sinful. The outspoken people involved in that particular sin explain that the person who condemned them cannot be a true Christian, because Jesus told his followers not to judge others. So, in light of this single verse, any person who would dare suggest that another person is sinning is labeled judgmental, unmerciful, and intolerant. "Judge not" is the rallying cry used to deflect any and all religious resistance to sinful lifestyles.

Unfortunately, Jesus' statements found in Matthew 7:1-5 have been conveniently lifted out of their context and twisted to suggest that it is always wrong to point out sin in others' lives. In truth, Jesus said no such thing. He said, "Judge not, that you be not judged. For with what judgment you judge, you will be judged" (5:1-2). He was simply saying that the criteria you use to measure sin in the lives of others will be the same criteria used to judge your life. In fact, Jesus went on to warn that a person should not look at the speck in his neighbor's eye when he has a beam or plank in his own eye. The problem in this context was not that a person saw sin (the speck) in his neighbor's eye; it was the fact that he missed his own, even bigger sin (the plank). Jesus' solution to the problem did not entail ignoring sin in one's neighbor. On the contrary, He said: "Hypocrite! First remove the plank from your own eye, and then you will see clearly to remove the speck out of your brother's eye" (5:5). Instead of Jesus declaring that all judgment is wrong, He was stating that judgment should be made only after one is willing to judge and correct his own sinful behaviors.

Other verses in the New Testament shed much light on the biblical concept of judging. In John

7:24, in defending His actions regarding healing a man on the Sabbath, Jesus stated: "Do not judge according to appearance, but judge with righteous judgment." Not only does Jesus not condemn all judgment in this verse, but He actually commands righteous judgment as a moral imperative for all.

> How is one to determine what type of judgment is righteous and what type is unrighteous?

What, then, would classify as "righteous judgment"? How is one to determine what type of judgment is righteous and what type is unrighteous? The New Testament gives two very clear statements regarding how to administer proper judgment. In John 5, Jesus explained the paramount characteristic of righteous judgment. He said, "I can of Myself do nothing. As I hear, I judge; and My judgment is righteous, because I do not seek My own will but the will of the Father who sent me." Simply put, righteous judgment must coincide with the will of God. To qualify that statement even further, Jesus commented, "He who rejects Me, and does not receive My words, has that which judges him—the word that I have spoken will judge him in the last day" (John

12:48). In a concise formula, righteous judgment must be consistent with God's will as found in His New Testament given through Jesus Christ.

This preliminary discussion of righteous judgment is a prerequisite to understanding and administering church discipline. First Corinthians 5 stands out as one of the most detailed set of instructions in the Bible pertaining to disfellowship. In that chapter, Paul instructed the Corinthian brethren to withdraw from one of their members who had his father's wife. Near the beginning of his discussion, Paul stated: "For I indeed, as absent in body but present in spirit, have already judged, as though I were present concerning him who has so done this deed" (5:3).

Paul had heard the evidence against the guilty man, weighed it against the teachings of Jesus (Matthew 19:1-9, Mark 10:1-12), and righteously judged the man guilty. Upon his correct judgment of the guilty man, he expected the Corinthians to use the same process to understand this man's guilt and remove him from their assembly. Paul issued no mealy-mouthed, half-hearted statement like, "We all have sin and therefore no one really has the right to say that anybody else is doing wrong."

Paul judged righteously as he was instructed by our Lord in John 7:24.

It is a distressing fact that many Christian men, especially in the United States, have been dissuaded from obeying God's command to disfellowship because it is not politically correct to judge others in any way. The usual rationale for failing to disfellowship based on the "we can't judge" idea goes something like this: "There is a person in our congregation who is known to (get drunk, use bad language, commit adultery, etc), but since none of us in the congregation is perfect, and we are not really supposed to judge others anyway, we will just ignore this sin and hope it goes away by itself."

Near the end of 1 Corinthians 5, Paul noted that withdrawal only applies to a person who is a Christian and cannot be extended to those in the world, "since then you would need to go out of the world." After making these statements, he asked two rhetorical questions: "For what have I to do with judging those also who are outside? Do you not judge those are inside?" (5:12). In answer to his first question, the rhetorical answer expected by the audience was, "Nothing, God will judge those outside the church" (which answer was supplied in verse 13). But the obvious and expected answer to the second question was, "Yes, we must judge those who are inside the Church."

> "If the world will be judged by you, are you unworthy to judge the smallest matters?"

Paul continued with this line of reasoning in chapter 6. He said that Christians were going to law against other Christians, which he viewed as an utterly disgraceful situation. This legal action between brethren occurred because the Corinthian Christians apparently did not think that any of their brethren were qualified to judge the cases. As evidence that such was not the case, Paul made two statements pertaining to Christians and judging. He said: "Do you not know that the saints will judge the world? And if the world will be judged by you, are you unworthy to judge the smallest matters? Do you not know that we shall judge angels? How much more the things that pertain to this life?" (1 Corinthians 6:2-3). While one would be hard pressed to explain fully the Christians' role in judging the world and angels, the point Paul is making is exceedingly clear—Christians have the capacity and God-ordained command to judge righteously. This righteous judgment certainly extends to being able to identify a sinning brother or sister and following God's instruction for the proper procedures for dealing with that sin, in an attempt to save the wayward Christian's soul.

Chapter 4

Discussion Questions

John 7:24

1. Are Christians to be totally "non-judgmental?" What does the media say about judging? What does the Bible say? Discuss times you have heard Matthew 7:1 used out of context.

2. Explain the term "righteous judgment." What criteria must be applied in order for judgment to be considered righteous? List and discuss some things that righteous judgment is not.

3. What did Jesus say would judge all people in the last day (John 12:48)? List several things that this fact should motivate people to do?

4. According to Paul, what categories of beings are the saints going to judge (1 Corinthians 6)? In what two ways were the Corinthians failing to judge righteously (chapters 5 and 6)?

5. Why do you think God instructs Christians to avoid taking other Christians to law? What relationship does this command have with righteous judgment?

Chapter 5
In the Name of Jesus Christ

Because of its severe nature, Paul put every ounce of authority available in the spiritual universe behind his command to withdraw from the sinning brother.

Chapter 5

> "In the name of our Lord Jesus Christ, when you are gathered together, along with my spirit, with the power of our Lord Jesus Christ, deliver such a one to Satan for the destruction of the flesh...."
> (1 Corinthians 5:4-5)

What is the first thing that comes to your mind when you hear the name Jesus Christ? For many, the name Jesus brings to mind a pale figure with long, perfectly combed brown hair, whose thin, weak body is shrouded in a white robe that stayed miraculously clean as He walked the dirty streets of first-century Palestine. When asked about His personality, many (Americans especially) think of a soft spoken, "mild" man who went about patting people on the back, telling them how much He loved them, never correcting or criticizing, and certainly never publicly denouncing sin in the life of an individual. Not that they think He did not denounce sin. Sure He would make some vague comments about avoiding sin that could be applied to just about anyone in his listening audience. But, in their minds, He would never say something as "unloving" as "John Smith is an adulterer and must repent or he will go to hell for eternity."

Thus, when people who do not properly understand the personality of Jesus approach the biblical command to withdraw fellowship, they generally ignore it, because they think it is not really something that Jesus would do.

In Matthew 28:18, the Bible says: "And Jesus came and spoke to them, saying, 'All authority has been given to Me in heaven and on earth.'" Colossians 3:17 teaches that "whatever you do in word or deed, do all in the name of the Lord Jesus, giving thanks to God the Father through Him." What does it mean to do everything "in the name of the Lord Jesus?" If a man off the street bangs on your door in the middle of the night and demands that you let him in, you call 911. But if a police officer, with a search warrant and a badge, knocks on your door at the same time of night and instructs you to open up "in the name of the law," then you let him in. Why? Because the police officer has been given the authority by the government to come into your house. But the stranger off the street has not been given that authority. The phrase "in the name of the law" means that the law gives him permission to compel you to open the door. If we do everything "in the name of the Lord Jesus," that means we do those things that Christ authorizes or commands us to do.

When we read Paul's statements concerning church discipline in First Corinthians 5, it is not surprising that the apostle calls the Corinthians to recognize the authority vested in Christ, and to disfellowship the adulterous brother "in the name of Jesus." Paul stated: "In the name of our Lord Jesus Christ, when you are gathered together, along with my spirit, with the power of our Lord Jesus Christ, deliver such a one to Satan for the destruction of the flesh…" (5:4-5).

> **That means we do those things that Christ authorizes or commands us to do.**

Admittedly, "delivering such a one to Satan" is an extremely harsh judgment that would demand more authority behind it than, "The men of the congregation think it's a pretty good idea." Because of its severe nature, Paul put every ounce of authority available in the spiritual universe behind his command to withdraw from the sinning brother.

The mental picture Paul paints for the church at Corinth is one in which the faithful brethren in Corinth approach the sinning brother, accompanied by the apostle Paul and the Lord Himself, and eject him from their assembly until such a time as he repents of his sin. Those who do not administer church discipline consistently and obediently often neglect to consider that Jesus Christ has demanded and commanded it to be done by His authority. Furthermore, in a spiritual sense, God has already withdrawn from the sinful brethren who should to be disfellowshiped. The line has been drawn in the spiritual sand, and the Godhead stands opposed to the one deserving to be disciplined. It is the heartbreaking truth that many otherwise faithful congregations stand opposed to God and squarely on the side of the wayward brother or sister by continuing to allow such blatant sin to go undisciplined.

Jesus confronted just such a situation in the beginning chapters of Revelation. In writing to the church at Pergamos, He commended them for their works and their admirable resistance in the face of severe persecution. In spite of that, Jesus said, "I have a few things against you, because you have there those who hold the doctrine of Balaam…. Thus you also have those who hold the doctrine of the Nicolaitans, which I hate. Repent, or else I will come to you quickly and will fight against them with the sword of my mouth" (Revelation 2:14-16). Please note that the entire congregation was told to repent. Yet, the whole church did not hold to the doctrine of Balaam or the Nicolaitans. What did Jesus have against the entire congregation? Is it not obvious that the congregation allowed such false teachers to be a part of their assemblies with little or no public censure? The brethren in Pergamos needed to repent of their failure to practice corrective public discipline, and the false teachers needed to repent of their wickedness.

Jesus Christ and all the authority of Heaven uphold church discipline. Since Jesus came to offer the abundant life to His followers, He understands that undisciplined sin grows like a cancer in the very spiritual bones of His bride, the church. Because of the love that He has for His bride, He knows that rebellious individuals who refuse to respond to His love must be disciplined publicly so that "all may fear." While He was on Earth, He attempted to dispel the notion that His teachings and His personality would not cause personal discomfort to attain the greater good. He boldly stated: "Do not think that I came to bring peace on earth. I did not come to bring peace but a sword. For I have come to 'set a man against his father, a daughter against her mother, and a daughter-in-law against her mother-in-law.' And a man's foes will be those of his own household" (Matthew 10:34-36).

> **He knows that rebellious individuals who refuse to respond to His love must be disciplined publicly so that "all may fear."**

In fact, the New Testament provides an amazingly pertinent example of Jesus' public denunciation of sin among His followers. In Matthew 16, Jesus asked His disciples who the crowds believed Him to be. The apostles explained that some thought He was John the Baptizer, others Elijah, and others thought Jesus was Jeremiah or one of the prophets. Jesus then asked the apostles who they thought He was. Peter spoke up and said, "You are the Christ, the Son of the living God" (16:16). Jesus praised Peter for his correct answer and stated that the confession and reality of Jesus' Deity would be the cornerstone on which the entire Church would be built. Immediately following this context detailing Peter's keen spiritual insight, Matthew's account notes that Jesus began to explain that He would suffer and die at the hands of the Jews. "Then Peter took Him aside and began to rebuke Him, saying, 'Far be it from You, Lord; this shall not happen to You!'" (16:22). It is at this point, that Mark's account of the episode says: "But when He (Jesus) had turned around and looked at His disciples, He rebuked Peter, saying, 'Get behind Me, Satan! For you are not mindful of the things of God, but the things of men'" (Mark 8:31). As much as Jesus loved Peter, public rebuke and censure in front of his disciples was necessary for Peter's own spiritual welfare as well as that of the other disciples.

Conclusion

Faithful followers of Christ who understand the personality of their Lord know that Jesus, because of His love, would wholeheartedly support Paul and the Corinthian brethren in their disciplinary actions of their wayward brother. And, in like fashion, every congregation of the Lord's church today who obeys the command to practice church discipline will do so with all the spiritual authority of Jesus Christ behind their actions.

Chapter 5
Discussion questions

1. Explain how a fundamental misunderstanding of the character of Jesus could cause people to avoid church discipline. Be sure to discuss our culture's view of the "love" of Jesus and the Bible's teaching on the subject.

2. How could Jesus have loved the Pharisees and still rebuked them as harshly as He did in places such as Matthew 23? Discuss how His statements in Matthew 23 relate to church discipline.

3. What does the Bible mean when it says that "all authority" has been given to Jesus (Matthew 28:18-20)? What does it mean to do all "in the name" of the Lord? How does this idea relate to other aspects of the Christian life such as acceptable worship?

4. In Matthew 16:16-18, Peter acknowledged Jesus as the Son of God. Why do you think the Bible records the fact that Jesus rebuked Peter immediately after that?

5. Why is purity in the church such an important issue with Christ? Describe the relationship that Christ has to the church. Fit verses like 2 Corinthians 11:2 and Ephesians 5:32 into your answer.

Chapter 6

The Fatal Flaw of Non-discipline

Satan has argued that the loving thing to do is to allow the wayward brother to remain in his condition so that you do not disturb his immediate 'happiness.'

Chapter 6

> "My son, do not despise the chastening of the Lord, nor detest His correction; for whom the Lord loves He corrects just as the son in whom he delights."
> (Proverbs 3:11-12)

Suppose a person went to the doctor for a yearly physical. During the routine examination, the doctor noticed several abnormal growths in one of the x-rays of the patient's lungs. Without mentioning the growths, the caring doctor asked to do some more tests. Upon further investigation, he confirmed that the patient had a very severe, malignant cancer that would most likely be terminal if it were not treated. This particular type of cancer, however, happened to be treatable, and more than half of those treated fully recovered. Aware of these statistics, the caring, concerned doctor decided not to inform the patient about the cancer. In fact, the doctor "loved" his patient so much that he did not want anything to interfere with the patient's peace of mind. After all, telling him he had terminal cancer would cause major mental and emotional anguish to this man. Just think what might occur. The patient might lose

That Their Souls Might Be Saved

his job, maybe even his wife, and this type of news could disrupt his present situation in all kinds of horrible ways. Because of the love and concern the doctor had for the patient, he told the man that everything was fine. He informed the dying man that there did not appear to be anything to worry about, that all was clear, and that he would look forward to seeing this healthy patient next year for his annual physical. The terminally ill patient walked out of the doctor's office completely confident in the physician's assessment, blissfully unaware that he would soon be dead.

Obviously, this scenario would hopefully never happen in a physical sense. Caring, concerned doctors do not find terminal cancer in their patients without fully informing them of the disease, and the various means available to treat the malady. If doctors did behave as the negligent physician mentioned above, they would be sued for every penny they had, and they certainly would not be considered caring, loving, or genuinely concerned for the well-being of their patients.

Yet, in a spiritual sense, it is all too common to see preachers, elders, and fellow church members who recognize cancerous sin in wayward brethren.

The Fatal Flaw of Non-discipline

But even though they recognize the sin, they watch the sinful brother spiraling toward eternity without confronting and informing him of the grim reality of his spiritual condition. One of the primary reasons for their silence is the fact that Satan has done a wonderful job convincing our society, and many in the church, that it is "unloving" to point out sin in others. On the contrary, Satan has argued that the loving thing to do is to allow the wayward brother to remain in his condition so that you do not disturb his immediate "happiness." After all, Satan pleads, God wants us to be happy, and confronting a brother about his sin would cause the poor soul untold mental and emotional grief. In fact, if he were to attempt to set his life right, it might cost him his job, his friends, and possibly even his family. Such an "unloving" action as confronting a brother or sister about sin finds no place in the modern, sentimental American churches that are known for their "love" and acceptance.

Defining correction and church discipline as "unloving" is not a new tactic. In fact, it seems that the Corinthians were carried away with a similar sentiment. Paul informed the Corinthian church that he had received information that one of their members was committing sexual immorality with his father's wife. He was shocked at their response to this situation. He stated: "And you are puffed up [or arrogant] and have not rather mourned, that he who has done this deed might be taken away from among you" (1 Corinthians 5:2). About what would the Corinthians be arrogant concerning this sinful brother? The Bible does not give us all the details, but it appears that the Corinthians were boasting of their love and acceptance of this man, even though he was blatantly committing sin. Their attitude seemed to be that by allowing this sinful brother to stay in their fellowship, they were proving that they truly loved him and would let nothing, not even his sin, stand in the way of their care for him. Paul's statement was designed to show that their negligent treatment of this brother's sin did not manifest the congregation's love for him, but actually was hindering the truly loving actions that would bring this man's soul back to Christ.

In truth, it is never the loving thing to do to

allow a brother or sister to continue in sin without correction or public discipline. Both the Old and New Testaments reveal the truth of this statement.

In Leviticus 19:17, Moses told the Israelites: "You shall not hate your brother in your heart. You shall surely rebuke your neighbor and not bear sin because of him." According to Moses, failing to rebuke a sinful neighbor was tantamount to hating that person. Yet, our society has convinced us that rebuking another person is an unloving action that no true Christian would do.

Proverbs 13:24 describes the same principle in the relationship of a parent with a child: "He who spares his rod hates his son, but he who loves him disciplines him promptly." Misguided parents today who refuse to correct and discipline their children because they "love them too much" have swallowed the false idea that discipline is unloving. Not only is discipline a loving action, but failure to discipline is manifest evidence that a parent hates his or her child. Thus, the Proverbs writer could rightly state: "My son, do not despise the chastening of the Lord, nor detest His correction; for whom the Lord loves He corrects just as the son in whom he delights" (Proverbs 3:11-12). The book of Hebrews expanded upon this theme: "If you endure chastening, God deals with you as with sons; for what son is there whom a father does not chasten? But if you are without chastening, of which all have become partakers, then you are illegitimate and not sons" (Hebrews 12:7-8). Not only does Hebrews explain that discipline is the a truely loving response to impenitent sin, the text also explains that, in the case of the child of God, it is evidence that God truly accepts the individual being disciplined as His child.

> **"If you endure chastening, God deals with you as with sons; for what son is there whom a father does not chasten?"**

One of the most interesting proofs of the fact that proper discipline is a truly loving action comes from the pen of the apostle Paul. In two instances in 2 Corinthians, he mentions that his reprimand of the congregation provided evidence of his love for them. In 2 Corinthians 2:4, Paul said, "For out of much affliction and anguish of heart I wrote to you, with many tears, not that you should be grieved, but that you might know the love which I have so abundantly for you."

The Fatal Flaw of Non-discipline

Paul condemned the sinful negligence of the Corinthian church and commanded them to withdraw their fellowship from their sinning brother. He openly rebuked their behavior, and the inspired letter in which he did so has been divinely preserved so that posterity can learn not to behave as the Corinthians did. And yet, Paul points to his statement of rebuke as evidence to the Corinthians of his abundant love for them. His rebuke proved his love! This idea stands in direct opposition to much that is taught and believed concerning public church discipline, today.

Again, in 2 Corinthians 7:8-12, Paul discussed the godly sorrow that afflicted the Corinthians and motivated them to obey his commands in the first letter. Their reaction to Paul's instructions was everything he had hoped for, and he concluded that they had proved themselves to be clear in the matter (7:11). Paul then offered a paramount reason for his original instructions "Therefore, although I wrote to you, I did not do it for the sake of him who had done the wrong, nor for the sake of him who suffered wrong, but that our care for you in the sight of God might appear to you" (7:12). Paul again offered his statement of rebuke and condemnation of a sinful activity in the Corinthian church as proof of his love and concern for the brother. In essence, Paul was explaining that he loved the brethren enough to tell them they were sinning and needed to change. Oh, that the Lord's church today had the kind of biblical love that would prove itself by the public rebuke of sin and the exercise of discipline when and where it is needed.

Conclusion

The mistaken notion that public church discipline is an "unloving," "judgmental" action does not find its origin in the Bible—quite the contrary. The Bible presents evidence which confirms that proper discipline is not only the loving action, but it provides proof of that love to the one being disciplined. The Bible makes it clear that discipline proves God's love for His children, parents' love for their children, and a congregation's love for its members. In reality, if a congregation wants to prove to its members that they do not love them, they should let the wayward continue in sin without discipline. If the elders or preacher desire to show the congregation that they do not love them, let them neglect their God-ordained

responsibility to preach and teach about church discipline. The fatal flaw of non-discipline is the idea that such negligence actually exhibits love. Nothing could be further from the truth. To stand idly by while a brother or sister plunges into the depths of sin, and sprawls toward eternal destruction, without taking the action God commanded to save such a lost soul surely cannot be construed as love. It must be recognized as spiritual criminal negligence. "Brethren, if anyone among you wanders from the truth, and someone turns him back, let him know that he who turns a sinner from the error of his way will save a soul from death and cover a multitude of sins" (James 5:19-20). The question comes to every congregation of the Lord's people, "Do we love our members enough to practice proper discipline?"

> The fatal flaw of non-discipline is the idea that such negligence actually exhibits love.

Chapter 6
Discussion Questions

1. Does God want us to be happy? Obedient? How do the two ideas relate? Cite verses that support your answer.

2. Why do many people think that it is an unloving act to rebuke a wayward brother or sister? What societal factors have affected this thought process?

3. How has a misunderstanding of "love" affected our society in areas such as parenting, school teaching, employer/employee relationships, welfare, etc?

4. Explain why rebuke and discipline actually are loving responses to sin. What does the Lord do to those He loves (Hebrews 12:3-11)? What provides proof that a parent does not love a child (Proverbs 13:24)? What does properly done church discipline prove to the one who is disciplined?

5. Those who do not properly administer church discipline often claim to be exhibiting love. What response did the Corinthians have to their sinful brother's lifestyle before Paul corrected them? Explain the importance of a person's soul above any other physical or emotional factors (Matthew 16:26). What part does the importance of the soul play in disfellowship?

Chapter 7
It Just Won't Work

Imagine the scenario if the patriarchs had operated by obeying only the commandments that they thought "would work."

It Just Won't Work

Chapter 7

> *"Behold, to obey is better than sacrifice, and to heed than the fat of rams. For rebellion is as the sin of witchcraft, and stubbornness as iniquity and idolatry."*
> (1 Samuel 15:22-23)

"Most congregations of the church of Christ in the United States don't even have true fellowship like the first century church. The various members often hardly know each other anyway. The majority of relationships between members are shallow, with little personal closeness. Since the church has little true fellowship, withdrawing fellowship is altogether ineffective—not to mention the fact that there are so many different congregations. The wayward member simply has to go a few miles down the road to a congregation that accepts his behavior. For these reasons, disfellowship does not accomplish the purpose of bringing the sinful brother back to Christ. It is a practice that once worked well for the close-knit early church but is virtually obsolete in the 21st century, especially in the United States."

In almost every congregation where disfellowship is seriously discussed, some members express sentiments like these. The argument is little more than rank pragmatism—if it works we do it; if it does not, we don't do it; disfellowship doesn't work, therefore, we don't do it. This common line of reasoning has two fundamental flaws: it completely ignores the nature of obedience, and it manifests a lack of faith in God's wisdom.

The Nature of Obedience

Both the Old and New Testaments are filled with explicit comments and illustrative examples that demonstrate the nature of obedience. If God commands something, it must be done exactly as He says.

One episode in King Saul's life perfectly illustrates this aspect of obedience. Due to the wickedness of the Amalekites, God ordered that the nation was to be decimated. He instructed King Saul to take the Israelite army and "go and attack Amalek, and utterly destroy all that they have, and do not spare them" (1 Samuel 15:3). God's command was clear and concise: destroy

It Just Won't Work

everything. Saul understood the command and set out to obey it. In fact, Saul did everything God commanded him—almost. Saul and his army destroyed the nation of Amalek, but "Saul and the people spared Agag and the best of the sheep, the oxen, the fatlings, the lambs, and all that was good, and were unwilling to utterly destroy them" (1 Samuel 15:9). Why would Saul and the people disobey such a direct command from God? Saul and his men neglected to recognize the nature of obedience. They second-guessed God's command. After all, how much sense does it make to destroy herds of excellent livestock? The cows, sheep, and lambs had not worshiped idols. The Amalekite livestock had done nothing that would "deserve" mass execution. Furthermore, it would be "inefficient" to destroy such good "innocent" livestock, since they could keep it and save the Israelites the trouble of raising their own. From a purely human standpoint, saving the Amalekite livestock made perfect sense. The only problem was, God told them to destroy it.

> **Saul and his men neglected to recognize the nature of obedience.**

When Saul encountered Samuel, the disobedient king said to him, "Blessed are you of the Lord! I have performed the commandment of the Lord" (1 Samuel 15:13). Samuel quickly pointed out Saul's error by asking why the noise of Amalekite livestock filled his ears. Saul retorted that "the people" wanted to save the best of the livestock to sacrifice to God. He was attempting to justify his disobedience by introducing a noble motive for his sin. But "noble" motives never justify disobedience to God's commands. Samuel said as much in his response to Saul: "Has the Lord as great delight in burnt offerings and sacrifices, as in obeying the voice of the Lord? Behold, to obey is better than sacrifice, and to heed than the fat of rams. For rebellion is as the sin of witchcraft and stubbornness as iniquity and idolatry" (15:22-23). Disobedience, regardless of motive or intent, is sinful rebellion.

> **"Behold, to obey is better than sacrifice, and to heed than the fat of rams."**

Imagine the scenario if the patriarchs had operated by obeying only the commandments that they thought "would work." The situation seems almost comical. God comes to Noah and tells him to build the ark in order to save his family from the ominous flood. Noah listens intently to God and begins to assess God's instructions. "I see, God, that the ark is supposed to have three decks. I'm not really sure having three decks is the best idea. After all, the wife and I are getting old, and going up and down all three decks might prove a little difficult. And it looks to me like we might not have enough ventilation. Furthermore, gopher wood is a little more difficult to work with than some of the pine woods I've used. And it doesn't seem to float as well as the others either. Thanks for the recommendations; I'll take them into consideration." Can you imagine such an attitude? Indeed not. The antithesis is attributed to Noah: "And Noah did according to all that the Lord commanded him" (Genesis 7:5; Hebrews 11:7). God commanded. Noah obeyed. And God saved Noah.

Envision God's exchange with Abraham if the father of the faithful had decided to do only those commands that he thought "would work." God comes to Abraham and commands him to sacrifice his son Isaac on Mt. Moriah. "God, I'm just not sure that's the best idea. You did say that through me all the nations would be blessed. And it is true that Isaac happens to be the son of promise through whom You intend to bless all nations. I really think that this sacrifice idea is not the best way to accomplish Your mission."

Such a dialogue did not take place. On the contrary, "Abraham stretched out his hand and took the knife to slay his son" (Genesis 22:10). Abraham was willing to do what God asked, regardless of how "effective" he thought the command was. He put his faith in the knowledge that God knew what was best.

Jesus attempted to explain the nature of obedience to His listeners, as well. At the end of the Sermon on the Mount, Jesus stated: "Not everyone who says to Me, 'Lord, Lord,' shall enter the kingdom of heaven, but he who does the will of My Father in heaven" (Matthew 7:21). Simply put, do what God says and you will be saved, do not obey God's commands and you will not. To explain more fully, Jesus noted: "Many will say to Me in that day, 'Lord, Lord, have we not prophesied in Your name, cast out demons in Your name, and done many wonders in Your name?'" (7:22). These people were working "for

Jesus." They were doing things that they thought would be acceptable to God. But they were not doing what God had commanded. Therefore, Jesus said to them: "And then I will declare to them, 'I never knew you; depart from Me, you who practice lawlessness!'" (7:23).

Acceptable obedience to God means doing what God says regardless of whether a person likes it or thinks it will work.

God Knows What He is Doing

The suggestion that disfellowship is no longer effective fails to recognize God's omniscience and His unsearchable depth of knowledge and wisdom. Isaiah wrote: "'For My thoughts are not your thoughts, nor are your ways My ways,' says the Lord. 'For as the heavens are higher than the earth, so are my ways higher than your ways, and my thoughts than your thoughts'" (Isaiah 55:8-9). Paul expressed similar inspired sentiments when he wrote: "Oh, the depth and the riches both of the wisdom and knowledge of God! How unsearchable are His judgments and His ways past finding out! For who has known the mind of the Lord? Or who has become His counselor? Or who has first given to Him and it shall be repaid to him? For of Him and through Him and to Him are all things, to whom be glory forever. Amen" (Romans 11:33-36).

Abraham summarized this idea in his rhetorical statement, "Shall not the judge of all the earth do right?" (Genesis 18:25). The necessary answer to his question is, "Of course God, the judge of all the earth, will do right." Let's apply that to disfellowship. Who would be in the best position to know the most effective way to bring a wayward member back to the fold? God, Who alone "searches the minds and hearts" (Revelation 2:23). Who would know what would be best for the health of a congregation and the church as a whole? Would it be sinful, weak humans or the God Whose ways are past finding out? To ask is to answer. The arrogant idea that modern members of the church have a better grasp on what would "work" regarding a wayward brother or sister stands opposed to everything the Bible says about God's infinitely superior wisdom. God knows best.

WHAT DO YOU MEAN BY WORK?

When some propose that disfellowship does not "work," they generally mean that church discipline does not guarantee that the wayward members will turn from their sin and repent. While it is true that disfellowship sometimes fails to "work" by bringing the wayward member back, it is not true that this "failure" is a flaw in the process. Consider the fact that many patients die during major heart surgery. Because of this fact, should all heart surgery be neglected because there is a chance that it will not work? Of course not. Additionally, God knows the best way to bring His children back, and church discipline is His designated plan to save them.

> God knows exactly what process is best to bring the wayward back to Him.

Futhermore, it is not the case that church discipline is solely aimed at bringing the wayward member back. It is also a gauge of the obedience of the group who is asked to implement it, as well as a deterrent to others who see the process done (see chapter 3). The failure in the process would be to neglect doing it.

Conclusion

Humans have never been given the prerogative to neglect commandments from God based on whether or not they think those commands are effective. God has commanded church discipline, and it is the church's responsibility to follow that command. God loves His children beyond human comprehension, and He knows exactly what process is best to bring the wayward back to Him. "Oh, the depth and the riches both of the wisdom and knowledge of God!"

Chapter 7

Discussion questions

1. Many people want to "serve" the Lord, but be on the "Board of Directors." Has this been true in the area of church discipline? How?

2. Discuss the aspects of acceptable obedience. Give several biblical examples of acceptable obedience and several of unacceptable obedience. Compare and contrast the two.

3. What aspects of congregational life in 21st-century American churches potentially hinder the effectiveness of church discipline? How can these be improved?

4. Will church discipline always be effect in bringing the sinful Christian back? Why or why not? Explain some aspects of discipline that "work" regardless of whether or not the sinful brother or sister repents.

5. Discuss the differences between God's thoughts and those of humans. Why is God in a much better position to know what "works?" What vested interest does God have in bringing the wanderer back?

Chapter 8

We Are Not Detectives

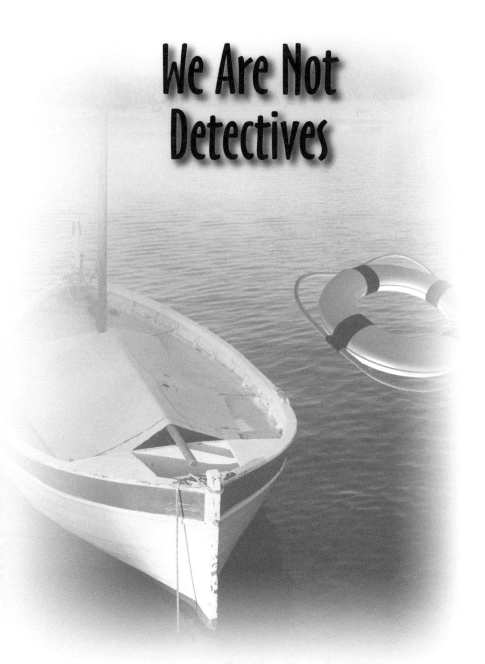

This 'don't ask, don't tell' policy is the rule in many congregations of the Lord's church.

Chapter 8

> "Test all things; hold fast what is good."
> (1 Thessalonians 5:21)

The scenario has been repeated countless times. Elders or leading men in a congregation will be informed that someone in their congregation is living in some type of sin. Many times this information will come from a brother or sister who has already discussed this personally with the sinful brother or sister. The leaders patiently listen to the report, and then calmly state that they have no firsthand knowledge of the situation. They further explain that they are not detectives, and it is not their job to investigate every member's life. Having made this statement, the case is often closed.

Statements like "we are not detectives" frequently mean much more than is explicitly stated. Some of those who make such statements simply do not want to know the truth about the situation. These men have a hunch that if they did ask a few questions, they would discover that the brother or sister is actually in a sinful state. Upon ascertaining this information, the men know that it would be their moral obligation to initiate the process of church discipline. Because they want to "keep the peace" and avoid "making any waves," they console themselves by thinking that they do not have firsthand information, and until they have such, they cannot move forward with any type of church discipline. Furthermore, there is little way that such "firsthand" information will come to them because they have decided not to discuss the situation with anyone, and certainly not to meet with the person who "allegedly" is living in sin. By not meeting with the member in a direct way, these men can counter every suggestion about this person's behavior by saying they have no "firsthand" knowledge of any sin, thus presumably absolving themselves of any responsibility in the situation. This "don't ask, don't tell" policy is the rule in many congregations of the Lord's church.

Unfortunately such an attitude of voluntary ignorance as to the spiritual state of the local flock shows a disregard for clear biblical principles manifested in the Old and New Testaments.

> Inquire, search out, and ask diligently.

In Deuteronomy 13, Moses outlined the procedure for dealing with all those who would attempt to entice the children of Israel away from worshiping God. In verses 6-11, Moses explained that any individual who tried to tempt his fellow Hebrews to worship idols was to be stoned. Moses went on to say that if someone reported that a certain city had been tempted to turn from God to idols, then the faithful Israelites were instructed to "inquire, search out, and ask diligently. And if it is indeed true and certain that such an abomination was committed among you, you shall surely strike the inhabitants of that city with the edge of the sword" (13:12-16). Notice the responsibility that the Israelites were given. If they heard such a report, they were not to believe it until they investigated the situation by diligently asking questions regarding the city. If, after their diligent inquiry, they discovered that the report was true, then they were instructed to take action. Such a course of action would make it impossible for the Israelites to remain willfully ignorant as to the spiritual condition of their cities.

Later, in Deuteronomy 17, Moses was inspired to make an almost identical statement, except that it applied to an individual instead of an entire city.

He wrote: "If there is found among you, within any of your gates which the Lord your God gives you, a man or a woman who has been wicked in the sight of the Lord your God, in transgressing His covenant…and it is told you, and you hear of it, then you shall **inquire diligently.** And if it is indeed true and certain that such an abomination has been committed in Israel, then you shall bring out to your gates that man or woman who has committed that wicked thing, and shall stone to death that man or woman with stones" (Deuteronomy 17:2-4, emp. added). Notice yet again that God placed on the Israelites the moral obligation to ascertain by diligent questioning whether the individual was indeed guilty or innocent. While it might have been rather easy to dismiss reports of "alleged" idol worship with the wave of a hand, due to a lack of "firsthand" information, such a course of action was not left open to the faithful Israelites.

Several years after Moses penned these commands, the Israelites were confronted with a national situation that called for the implementation of these principles. The tribes of Reuben, Gad, and half of Manasseh had finished their tour of duty by helping their fellow tribes conquer the land

We Are Not Detectives

of Canaan. Moses had promised these two and a half tribes land on the eastern side of the Jordan River if they would faithfully fight alongside their fellow Israelites until the land was conquered. Joshua dismissed these men to return to their homes and their cattle. Upon their return, these tribes built a "great, impressive altar" near the bank of the Jordan. Fearing that these two tribes were apostatizing, "the whole congregation of the children of Israel gathered together at Shiloh" intending to go to war with the wayward tribes. Before they took such drastic measures, however, they sent a delegation composed of Phinehas the priest and ten rulers, one from each of the remaining tribes. This delegation was sent to bring the separated tribes to their senses. Upon arriving at the scene, the delegation learned that the tribes were not sinning, nor were they intending to leave the worship of Jehovah God. They had built the altar so that they would have a bond with the ten tribes on the other side of the Jordan, and so that their descendants would be recognized as Israelites who worshiped God instead of idols. Upon hearing this heartening news, Phinehas and the delegation reported back to the Israelites. "So the thing pleased the children of Israel, and the children of Israel blessed God" (Joshua 22:32-33). Thus, the ten tribes proved that they were faithful to God's commands to diligently inquire as to the truth of reports of apostasy, and their national unity increased because of their faithfulness.

The New Testament contains statements that teach similar principles of inquiry as those found in the Old Testament. In Acts 20, Paul called the Ephesian elders to come to him at Miletus. Verses 17-38 of that chapter narrate one of the most touching, emotional scenes in the book of Acts. Paul recounted to the elders his faithful behavior towards them. He also warned them that "savage wolves" would come in "not sparing the flock." Sadly, the wolves would come from among themselves. Due to this dangerous situation, Paul said to those elders (and subsequently all elders and leaders of congregations): "Therefore watch, and remember that for three years I did not cease to warn everyone night and day with tears" (Acts 20:31). What did Paul mean when he warned them to "watch?" Such a statement would mean to pay very close attention to what was being taught and practiced among their flock. How would elders know what was being taught and practiced unless they were willing to diligently inquire into the teachings and actions of those in their flocks? Here again, we see that it is a moral obligation of a congregation's leadership to make sure that they know the spiritual state of the flock.

In his concluding remarks in First Thessalonians, Paul made a statement that exemplifies the principle of inquiry. He wrote, "Test all things; hold fast what is good" (5:21). While this is a very general command that would apply to various aspects of doctrine and actions, it certainly would apply to a church leadership's responsibility to "test" the lives of the flock by inquiring into reports and suspicions of sinful behavior.

> It is a moral obligation to make sure that leaders know the spiritual state of the flock.

Jesus' comments to the seven churches of Asia contained principles that relate to this discussion as well. Jesus had a few things against the church at Pergamos, because they had those among them who maintained the doctrine of Balaam, who taught, among other things, that certain forms of sexual immorality were acceptable. Also, some in Pergamos held to the teachings of the Nicolaitans, which the Lord hated. The church at Pergamos should have tested these individuals by ascertaining the tenets of their teachings and comparing them to the New Testament teachings. They should have diligently inquired into the lives of those committing sexual immorality and realized that such actions were not in accord with Christ's teachings. They had failed to "test all things" and were reprimanded quite severely by the Lord for their lack of diligence.

Conclusion

It is the moral obligation of every eldership in every congregation to watch out for their flock by inquiring into legitimate reports of alleged sinfulness. In many happy instances, such reports will prove to be false, and no action will need to be taken. In other instances, the report will prove true, and action will be required. Willful ignorance as to the sinfulness of a person's lifestyle will not excuse leaders from their obligation to diligently inquire into the reports of sinful behavior. And while it is true that such inquiries will have certain limits, and leaders are not obligated to hire private investigators or stake out the houses of those accused of sin, they cannot ignore such situations. Often times a simple meeting with the person accused will bring to light the truth. It is amazing that many of these "simple" meetings never take place, due to the fact that the truth is sometimes less valuable to those leading a congregation than are the "calm waters" of the status quo where the "peace" is kept, and no one's feathers are ruffled.

CHAPTER 8

DISCUSSION QUESTIONS

1. Why do you think it is easier not to want to know the facts in some cases? How effective is an "ignorance" plea without proper inquiry into the situation?

2. List and discuss some biblical examples of situations in which sin was alleged to have occurred. What principles can be gleaned from such examples?

3. Discuss attitudes that would lead to willful ignorance. What factors in a congregation could cause such attitudes to creep in? How could such attitudes be eliminated or avoided?

4. What attitude should faithful men and women have concerning alleged sin? Why is accurate knowledge of alleged sin so important? Discuss what can occur when legitimate reports of sin are ignored.

5. How should biological family relationships factor into the withdrawal process? Be sure to include verses such as Deuteronomy 13:6-10 and Matthew 12:46-50 in your discussion.

Chapter 9
This Is Going To Hurt

The tremendous amount of love required to correctly discipline a sinful brother or sister cannot eliminate the acute pain caused by the process.

Chapter 9

> "Now no chastening seems to be joyful for the present, but grievous...."
> (Hebrews 12:11)

Like a shot from the doctor, a spanking from a loving parent, or a root canal from the dentist, church discipline hurts. There is absolutely no way to avoid the pain inherent in the process. In fact, it is the pain of the procedure that generally keeps people from administering it. It hurts, and it hurts badly. And it is not just the sinful brother who feels the pain. The entire congregation grieves and aches during the painful process. When one member of the body suffers, the entire body feels the pain (1 Corinthians 12:26). In a spiritual sense, it is as if a part of the body is being severed without anesthesia.

Such is the nature of proper discipline. It only works if it is powerful enough to cause grief, pain, or sorrow. The Hebrews writer explained: "Now no chastening seems to be joyful for the present, but grievous...." (12:11). There is nothing fun about chastening and discipline, and it seems grievous while it is happening. The Proverbs writer noted: "Blows that hurt cleanse away evil, as do stripes the inner depths of the heart" (20:30). The key phrase in the proverb is "hurt." Blows that do not hurt accomplish nothing. They are altogether ineffective in any effort to change behavior. In many cases, it is only the painful discipline that has corrective power. The tremendous amount of love required to correctly discipline a sinful brother or sister cannot eliminate the acute pain caused by the process.

> "Before I was afflicted I went astray, but now I keep Your word...."

Obviously, the pain is intended by God to wake the wayward brother from his spiritual slumber and force him back into the reality of his lost condition. The psalmist once wrote: "Before I was afflicted I went astray, but now I keep Your word.... It is good for me that I have been afflicted, that I may learn Your statutes" (Psalm 119:67, 71). Spiritual and emotional pain is a valuable tool that has the power to prick the heart and bring about repentance.

In Acts 2, the Bible describes a situation in which the painful recognition of sin brought about godly sorrow that produced repentance. On the Day of Pentecost following the resurrection of Christ, Peter and the other apostles stood before the crowd in Jerusalem miraculously speaking to various nationalities in their own languages. In the process of this Gospel sermon presented by Peter and recorded in Acts 2, Peter told his listeners they had taken the Son of God "by lawless hands," crucified Him, and put Him to death (2:23). Upon coming to the realization of the terrible nature of their sin, at least 3,000 of the listeners "were cut to the heart" and asked Peter and the other apostles what they needed to do. The phrase "cut to the heart" indicates the severe emotional pain felt by the "chastened" crowd. They had done wrong. Peter had explained to them the nature of their sin. And they were painfully aware of their criminal, sinful, rebellious behavior. Their grief-stricken hearts cried out through the pain for a balm that would soothe the emotional and spiritual torment their souls were suffering. That balm was freely offered to them through obedience to the Gospel plan of salvation, which included their repentance and immersion in water for the forgiveness of their sins. Upon compliance with

Peter's instructions, their pain and grief turned to joy when they "gladly received" the words of Peter (2:40). The pain intentionally inflicted through Peter's loving but bold sermon accomplished its mission of spiritual health and healing that eclipsed the grief it inflicted.

This same curative use of pain is evident in Paul's dealing with the Corinthian church concerning church discipline. In 2 Corinthians 2:3-10, Paul seems to be clearly referring to the disciplinary actions that he had previously commanded in 1 Corinthians 5. In this second epistle, Paul said: "For out of much affliction and anguish of heart I wrote to you, with many tears, not that you should be grieved, but that you might know the love which I have so abundantly for you." First, it is interesting to notice that Paul says that by writing to the Corinthians instructing them to practice church discipline, he was proving to them that he loved them enough to tell them the truth and to help them purify themselves. Second, notice that Paul was grieved by having to command church discipline. His quill and papyrus were figuratively (possibly literally) stained with the many tears that he had cried over this wayward brother and the pain that his sin had caused the entire congregation. Since the pain was not limited to the sinner, but was indeed experienced by the congregation, Paul continued: "But if anyone has caused grief, he has not grieved me, but all of you to some extent—not to be too severe" (2:5). One member of the body was causing pain that shot through the entire body.

> We loved them enough to tell them the truth and to help them purify themselves.

In 2 Corinthians 7:8-12, the church's response to Paul's correction in his first epistle seems to be clearly under discussion. Upon informing the Corinthians of their need to repent and take action, the church members became extremely sorrowful. They were grieved at their sin and the improper way that they had handled the situation prior to Paul's first letter. Upon hearing of their sinful neglect, their grief became intense. Concerning this situation, Paul wrote: "For even if I made you sorry with my letter, I do not regret it; though I did regret it. For I perceive that the same epistle made you sorry, though only for a while. Now I rejoice, not that you were made sorry, but that your sorrow led to repentance. For you were made sorry in a godly manner, that you might suffer loss from us in nothing. For godly sorrow produces repentance to salvation, not to be regretted; but the sorrow of the world produces death. For observe this very thing, that you sorrowed in a godly manner…. In all things you proved yourselves to be clear in this matter" (2 Corinthians 7:8-11).

The pain and grief felt by the Corinthian church caused them to repent of their sinful behavior, align their actions with the commands of God, and implement the procedure described by Paul in 1 Corinthians. This godly sorrow brought about repentance that led to a complete clearing of the Corinthians in everything concerning the actions commanded by God. Just like a shot that hurts momentarily but can fight disease for months or years, their sorrow lasted only for a moment, and it turned into joy.

THE OPPOSITE RESPONSE TO PAIN

Unfortunately, not all corrective discipline is applied to those who are willing to be improved by it. The Hebrews writer said that chastening (or discipline) "yields the peaceable fruit of righteousness to those who **have been trained by it**" (12:11). Not every person has an honest heart that is trained by discipline. It is the sad truth that sometimes, the pain that is designed to bring about repentance is twisted by the victim to bring about further rebellion and spiritual decay.

Such was the case with Stephen's listeners in Acts 7. He preached a sermon like Peter's in Acts 2, explaining to the Jewish leaders that they had crucified the Son of God. He informed them that they were stubborn and stiff-necked, refusing to heed the instructions of the Holy Spirit by obeying the teachings of Christ. The Bible then explains that these men were "cut to the heart" just as those in Acts 2 had been (7:54). Yet, this pointed pricking of the listeners' consciences in Acts 7 did not bring repentance or an inquiry into what they needed to do in order to be pleasing to God. On the contrary, they used this pain to spur them on in their vicious deed of stoning Stephen. The pain that had softened the hearts of those on the Day of Pentecost had hardened the hearts of Steven's listeners.

> **Not every person has an honest heart that is trained by discipline.**

Paul explained this same situation to the Corinthians when he stated that "godly sorrow produces repentance to salvation, not to be regretted; but the sorrow of the world produces death" (2 Corinthians 7:10). The same discipline administered to different people will cause some to repent and become obedient to God's commands (as the Corinthians had done), but will cause others to harden their hearts and commit even greater acts of rebellion against their Creator.

Conclusion

The process of disciplining a sinful brother or sister is inherently painful. Not only does the one being disciplined feel the pain, but it affects the entire congregation. There is nothing pleasant about church discipline. The potential benefits of the process, however, outweigh the grief and sorrow that are felt temporarily. And, while some will choose to harden their hearts due to this painful discipline, others will allow it to turn their hearts to godly sorrow that produces repentance. They will allow themselves to be trained by the discipline to yield the peaceable fruit of righteousness.

Chapter 9
Discussion questions

1. What emotional consequences are naturally involved in the disciplinary process? Even though pain brings discomfort, is that necessarily a bad thing?

2. Discuss ways that pain can be beneficial in our everyday lives. In our emotional lives. In our spiritual lives.

3. List and discuss biblical examples in which two different responses occurred in the hearts of those who were painfully rebuked in some way. Compare and contrast the attitudes of each group.

4. How can a congregation effectively demonstrate to the disciplined Christian that they, too, are experiencing pain in the process? List and discuss specific ways.

5. Discuss times in your personal life when you have been "pricked to the heart" by something you read or heard from God's Word. What type of response did you exhibit?

Chapter 10

When The Wayward Return

When a wayward sinner comes back to the fold, the entire congregation must sincerely forgive him or her.

Chapter 10

> "This punishment which was inflicted by the majority is sufficient for such a man, so that, on the contrary, you ought rather to forgive and comfort him, lest perhaps such a one be swallowed up with too much sorrow."
> (2 Corinthians 2:6-8)

From reading the Bible, one quickly learns that God rejoices greatly when those who are lost repent. The parables found in Luke 15 of the lost sheep, lost coin, and lost son vividly portray the idea that the Father's heart is thrilled by the restoration of His children. Among the saddest pictures presented in the Bible is that of Christ agonizing over impenitent Jerusalem. Most likely with tears streaming down His face, Christ cried: "O Jerusalem, Jerusalem, the one who kills the prophets and stones those who are sent to her! How often I wanted to gather your children together, as a hen gathers her brood under her wings, but you were not willing" (Luke 13:34). In truth, God is "not willing that any should perish but that all should come to repentance" (2 Peter 3:9).

Ultimately, one of the primary goals of church

discipline is to bring the wayward sinner back to the fold. God searches the hearts of men and knows the most productive way to persuade them to obedience. His ordained procedure of congregational discipline provides an essential cog in the spiritual machinery He has designed to bring the wayward to repentance. Church discipline works to bring back the lost. Not always, but much of the time, it accomplishes what other, less stringent procedures cannot—it jolts the erring brother or sister back to spiritual reality. Often, the disciplined brother or sister returns with a contrite, penitent heart, seeking mercy and forgiveness for his or her sins. Their repentance not only brings them back into fellowship with God and the congregation, but it often prevents them from inflicting further pain on themselves.

What should be the response of the congregation who has disciplined one of its members when that member repents? The answer is obvious to any person familiar with the Spirit of Christ. The penitent member should be welcomed back into

> Church discipline works to bring back the lost.

the fold with open arms, and his sinful behavior should be put in the past so that it no longer affects his relationship with his brothers and sisters. The apostle Paul said as much when he wrote his second letter to the Corinthians. In a passage that clearly seems to be referring to the Corinthians' obedience in disciplining their brother who had his father's wife, Paul wrote: "This punishment which was inflicted by the majority is sufficient for such a man, so that, on the contrary, you ought rather to forgive and comfort him, lest perhaps such a one be swallowed up with too much sorrow. Therefore I urge you to reaffirm your love to him" (2 Corinthians 2:6-8).

The Corinthian church had been hurt by the sinful brother. Their inadequate response to his sin had caused them to feel the sharp rebuke of the inspired apostle Paul. Upon learning what they needed to do, they wasted no time in withdrawing from this brother. This disciplinary process caused the brother to soften his heart, repent, and come back to the fold, exactly as it was designed to do. Yet, it seems that the congregation might not have been receiving the man back as quickly as they had withdrawn from him. Paul's instructions indicate that the Corinthians needed to forgive the brother, reaffirm their love for him, and welcome him back into the congregation with open arms. It is interesting to note that failure to obey these instructions to lovingly forgive the brother had the potential to cause him to be "swallowed up with too much grief." In essence, failing to forgive the brother could be just as detrimental to his spiritual condition as failure to discipline him.

To discuss forgiveness to any degree of completeness would require a separate book in and of itself. However, some of the important themes must be understood as they pertain to church discipline. When people are hurt by another, there is a natural tendency to be angry and seek retribution for the pain inflicted. Jesus, however, has instructed all of His followers to leave vengeance to the Lord and to forgive their enemies and those who sin against them. In the model prayer, Jesus told His followers to pray, "Forgive us our debts, as we forgive our debtors" (Matthew 6:12). In an explanatory note at the end of the prayer, Jesus said: "For if you forgive men their trespasses, your heavenly Father will also forgive you. But if you do not forgive men their trespasses, neither will your Father forgive your trespasses" (6:14-15).

To illustrate His point more vividly, Jesus told the parable of the unforgiving servant. This wicked man owed his master an exorbitant amount of money. He could not pay it, so his merciful master forgave him. The servant then went and found a fellow servant who owed him an insignificant amount. His fellow servant could not pay, so the unforgiving servant had him thrown in jail. When the master heard about the servant's wickedness he "was angry and delivered him to the torturers until he should pay all that was due him." Immediately after telling the parable, Jesus explained, "So My heavenly Father also will do to you if each of you, from his heart, does not forgive his brother his trespasses" (Matthew 18:21-35). When a wayward sinner comes back to the fold, the entire congregation must sincerely forgive him or her. This forgiveness accomplishes two things. First, it encourages the wayward Christian and manifests the love of Christ. Second, it opens the heart of God to forgive the sins of those in the congregation, since their own

> **When a wayward sinner comes back to the fold, the entire congregation must sincerely forgive him.**

forgiveness depends on their merciful reaction to the penitent one.

Another important aspect of forgiveness involves the number of times a person (or congregation) is required to forgive the penitent brother or sister. Along these lines, Peter asked the pertinent questions: "Lord, how often shall my brother sin against me, and I forgive him? Up to seven times?" Jesus' answer stressed the unlimited nature of forgiveness. He responded to Peter: "I do not say to you, up to seven times, but up to seventy times seven" (Matthew 18:21-22). As often as the erring Christian is willing to repent, a congregation should be willing to extend their loving arms of forgiveness.

A Test of Obedience

In truth, church discipline is not only an effective procedure to bring the wandering Christian back, it also acts as a way to test the obedience of a congregation. In the context of urging the Corinthians to reaffirm their love to the penitent sinner, Paul wrote, "For to this end I also wrote, that I might put you to the test, whether you are obedient in all things" (2 Corinthians 2:9).

How the congregation handled the instructions to discipline the wayward brother, and to forgive him upon his repentance, would manifest their obedience to God's commands. Failure to properly discipline or forgive the brother would prove that the Corinthians were not obedient to God's commands. Were we to apply such a test to many modern congregations of the Lord's church, it seems that many would sadly fail this biblical test of obedience.

The elders of Collinsville church of Christ in Oklahoma who disfellowshiped Marian Guinn conducted themselves in a most biblical and obedient way when it came to the forgiveness aspect of the discipline they implemented. Upon initially hearing that the courts had charged the congregation to pay Marian $390,000 for damages, *Time Magazine* quoted Roy Witten, one of the elders of the congregation as saying, "If Marian were to come back tomorrow, we would welcome her with open arms and the angels in heaven would join with us" (*Time*, 1984, March 26). Oh, that God's people would have such a heart in them (Deuteronomy 5:9).

Chapter 10
Discussion questions

1. What attitude should a congregation exhibit when a disciplined Christian repents and returns? List some improper responses. What could happen if a congregation fails to respond correctly?

2. What factors influence a wayward Christian's repentance? How does a congregation's response affect each individual member's relationship with God? Be sure to include passages like Matthew 6:14-15 and 18:21-35 in your discussion.

3. Why is forgiveness such a difficult spiritual discipline to practice? List and discuss the various emotions that occur when sin causes division in a relationship.

4. God's command to forgive is what kind of test? Pinpoint areas in your personal life in which you are being tested. How will identifying these challenging areas help in your spiritual journey?

5. List and discuss several biblical examples of those who passed the test of forgiveness. Those who did not. Compare and contrast the two.

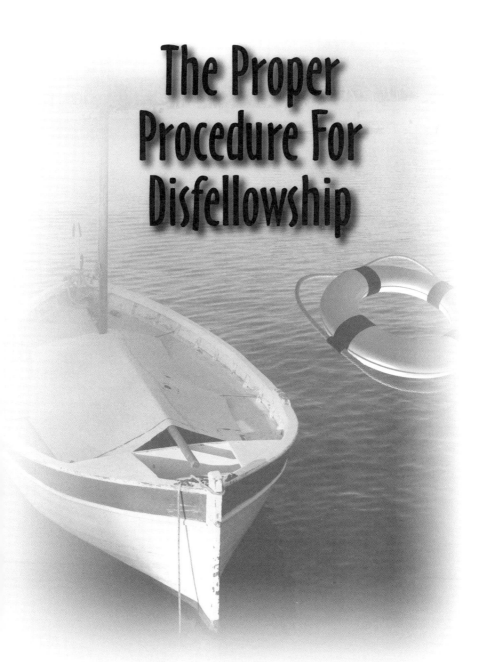

Chapter 11

The Proper Procedure For Disfellowship

It must be remembered, however, that just because specific procedural steps have not been given for every single case, that is no reason to avoid the command to practice discipline.

Chapter 11

> "And if he refuses to hear them, tell it to the church. But if he refuses even to hear the church, let him be to you like a heathen and a tax collector."
> (Matthew 18:17)

The Bible clearly teaches that church discipline is mandatory for any faithful congregation of the Lord's people. Once a congregation realizes the importance of this command, several questions will naturally surface. One of the first questions will most likely be about the proper procedure for the discipline of wayward brothers or sisters. Should the sinful brother or sister be visited and informed about what is happening? How many times should the wayward be visited before the actual discipline takes place? Should withdrawal happen in a public or private setting? Should the elders, family members, deacons, or close friends be the ones who play the principal role in the withdrawal? These and many other procedural questions are almost certain to arise. Therefore, a look at several foundational aspects of this process is in order.

Jesus' Instructions in Matthew 18:15-17

One of the first passages that comes to mind in a discussion of disciplinary procedure is Matthew 18:15-17. The text reads:

"Moreover if your brother sins against you, go and tell him his fault between you and him alone. If he hears you, you have gained your brother. But if he will not hear you, take with you one or two more, that 'by the mouth of two or three witnesses every word may be established.' And if he refuses to hear them, tell it to the church. But if he refuses even to hear the church, let him be to you like a heathen and a tax collector."

Jesus' instructions here can be applied to situations in which one brother has been done wrong by another brother. Maybe a brother has embezzled some money from his fellow Christian, or slandered him and damaged his reputation. The procedure for dealing with a brother who has personally sinned against another is quite straightforward. First, the brother who has been wronged is instructed to visit the sinner. If that does not work, he should take one or two more people with him to visit the wayward brother. If that still does not work, the congregation as a whole should be informed. And if the collective influence of the congregation remains ineffective in eliciting the repentance of the wayward, he should be disciplined.

The Collinsville elders used these procedural guidelines when they withdrew from Marian Guinn. And these steps can function as an excellent framework that embodies the key principles for all cases of church discipline.

> **If the influence of the congregation remains ineffective in eliciting the repentance of the wayward, he should be disciplined.**

These procedures, however, seem to be dealing with a specific case in which an individual brother in the congregation has been wronged by another brother. They do not seem to be dealing specifically with other instances that might call for disciplinary action such as when a brother or sister might be involved in the public teaching of false doctrine or widely known adultery. For instance, when Paul wrote to the Corinthians concerning the Christian who had his father's wife, he simply instructed the church to withdraw from the wayward brother. From a straight forward reading of the text (1 Corinthians 5:1-13), Paul does not seem to include any preliminary meetings with the sinner involving individual members of the congregation. In fact, although Paul was absent, he did not feel the need to meet personally with the brother himself. Apparently, the sin was of such a public nature by the time Paul was informed, immediate action was necessary. Let's note a few of the salient points regarding the church's action.

> **The public nature of church discipline accomplishes at least two very important things.**

CHURCH DISCIPLINE SHOULD BE PUBLIC

When Paul addressed the Corinthians about the disciplinary action needed to correct their situation, he insisted that withdrawing from the wayward brother should be a public matter, in the presence of the entire congregation. He wrote: "In the name of our Lord Jesus Christ, when you are gathered together, along with my spirit, with the power of our Lord Jesus Christ, deliver such a one to Satan for the destruction of the flesh…" (1 Corinthians 5:4-5). The public nature of the process was also alluded to by Jesus when He taught that "the church" should be informed about the impenitent brother. The public nature of church discipline accomplishes at least two very important things. First, it helps keep the church pure and discourages others from sinning in a similar way (as discussed in chapter three). Second, it brings to bear on the sinful brother or sister a collective pressure that could not otherwise be produced.

In addition to the public denunciation of the sinful behavior of the wayward, Paul extended the process to include refraining from eating with the brother. There is some discussion here as to whether verses 9-13 deal with the fellowship meal that involved the entire congregation or whether Paul was instructing individuals to refrain from eating with the sinful brother. While the context seems to lean more toward the view that the entire congregation should avoid eating with the sinful brother, the principle would also seem to extend to individuals as well. The point being, if a Christian is involved in a soul-condemning sin, then his fellow Christians should not ignore the sin and continue to interact with him in ways that would seem to convey an attitude of apathy toward his sin. In 2 Thessalonians 3:14-15, Paul wrote: "And if anyone does not obey our word

That Their Souls Might Be Saved

in this epistle, note that person and do not keep company with him, that he may be ashamed. Yet do not count him as an enemy, but admonish him as a brother." While total avoidance of the wayward brother is not necessarily instructed, it is the case that contact with the sinning brother or sister should be confined to interaction that would bring to mind the guilty party's sin and constantly urge the impenitent party to return to the fold.

For instance, suppose two members of the local congregation regularly meet to play golf on Tuesday afternoons. One of the two commits adultery and is disfellowshiped by the congregation. What should be the response of his fellow Christian in reference to his relationship to this brother? Should he continue to play golf with him on Tuesdays? From applying the principles set forth by Paul, it seems that the best procedure would be to discontinue his recreational relationship with the wayward brother until he repents. It would be appropriate, and in line with the spirit of proper church discipline, however, for the faithful brother to send the wayward Christian a card or e-mail, or give him a call, expressing the idea that he is still loved, and that the faithful brother would love to continue their relationship if and when the sinning brother returns to Christ.

Other Passages to Consider

Numerous other passages offer information about withdrawing from sinful brethren. In 2 Thessalonians 3:6, Paul instructed the church there: "But we command you, brethren, in the name of our Lord Jesus Christ, that you withdraw from every brother who walks disorderly and not according to the tradition which he received from us." In this passage, no clear procedure is described by which the Thessalonians should proceed to withdraw from the disorderly. It seems that the elders of the church were left to decide many of the specifics themselves that were consistent with Jesus' instructions.

> **Paul told the young preacher Titus to "reject a divisive man after the first and second admonition."**

Paul told the young preacher Titus to "reject a divisive man after the first and second admonition, knowing that such a person is warped and sinning, being self-condemned" (Titus 3:10-11). To the "elect lady," the apostle John wrote: "If anyone comes to you and does not bring this doctrine, do not receive him into your house nor greet him; for he who greets him shares in his evil deeds" (2 John 10-11). In his third epistle, John denounced Diotrephes, who loved to have the prominent position in the church (3 John 9-12). In addition, Paul withstood Peter to his face when he was showing favoritism to the Jewish Christians (Galatians 2:11-14), and delivered the blasphemous Hymenaeus and Alexander to Satan, a statement that brings to mind his instructions to the Corinthians to do the same to their adulterous brother (1 Timothy 1:20).

Conclusion

It seems that there could exist many instances in which discipline would be necessary. The procedure set forth by Jesus in Matthew 18:15-17 would be the wisest place to begin, and can form a standard that provides necessary principles for any procedures enforced by a congregation. Necessarily, some of the specific aspects regarding church disciplinary procedures will be left up to the eldership. It must be remembered, however, that just because specific procedural steps have not been given for every single case, that is no reason to avoid the command to practice discipline. For instance, the

Bible does not tell us exactly how to partake of the Lord's Supper. Should we pass a tray? Should we put it on a table and all walk up front and take the bread and juice from it? Should we eat it in the morning, middle of the day, or evening, etc? Lack of specific information along these lines would never lead us to conclude that we should simply stop taking the Lord's Supper on the first day of the week, because we are not sure whether to pass it in a tray or put in on a table. Neither should the lack of specific information regarding every possible circumstance of church discipline lead us to forsake the command and avoid implementing the practice in our churches.

Chapter
11
Discussion questions

1. List and discuss several of the most important verses that give procedural guidelines for withdrawal. In your own words, explain the steps that are outlined in these verses about withdrawal.

2. Why do you think that God instructs us to impose church discipline when we are "gathered together?" Identify factors that make such "public" discipline more effective?

3. What specific function did Paul instruct the Corinthian Christians to refrain from doing with the sinful brother? List and discuss some qualities that make this event special.

4. What details about the withdrawal procedure are not outlined in the Bible? Why do you think this is the case? In areas without specific commands, what should be done?

5. Because some specifics are not given, what inappropriate response have some churches exhibited toward the entire disciplinary process? Why is this an improper response?

CHAPTER 12

What Sins Would Call For Withdrawal?

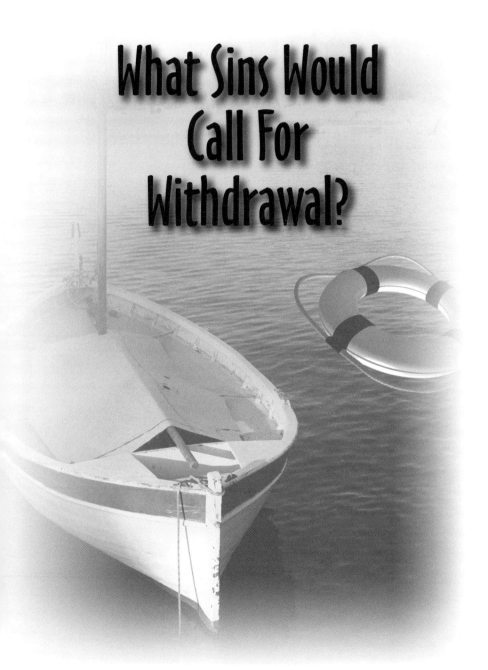

Any Christian who persists in a rebellious, sinful lifestyle in spite of proper instruction, after being admonished and lovingly warned to repent, should be disciplined.

Chapter 12

> "But now I have written to you not to keep company with anyone named a brother, who is a fornicator, or covetous, or an idolater, or a reviler, or a drunkard, or an extortioner—not even to eat with such as person."
> (1 Corinthians 5:11)

As stated in the previous chapter, certain questions naturally arise when a congregation decides it will begin to follow God's command to practice church discipline. One of the most frequently asked questions has to do with what type of sins would be grounds for public church discipline. Should a family be withdrawn from for forsaking the assembly for several months? Should a person in an adulterous relationship be disfellowshiped? Would sins such as gossip or habitual lying be grounds for discipline? As was the case in the last chapter, not every question along these lines can be answered definitively. The New Testament does, however, specify several sins that would demand discipline. The Scriptures also set forth several principles upon which grounds church discipline can be determined.

SEXUAL SIN

When Paul wrote his first epistle to the Corinthians, the case of the adulterous relationship of the brother who had his father's wife was so well-known that it had reached Paul hundreds of miles away. The Corinthians not only were not ashamed of the situation, but they had somehow found a reason to boast that this man was in their assembly. Upon hearing of this adulterous union, Paul called for the immediate public withdrawal of the Corinthians from this sexually immoral brother. Paul then explained that God did not want the Corinthians to "keep company with" any brother who was known to engage in sexual misconduct (1 Corinthians 5:9-11). It is clear, then, that sexually illicit relationships, if known to a congregation, are grounds for immediate withdrawal. In our 21st century congregations, this situation would primarily concern couples who have been divorced for some reason other than adultery, but have remarried without scriptural grounds, and are living in adulterous unions even though our culture might consider these unions

> It is clear, then, that sexually illicit relationships, if known to a congregation, are grounds for immediate withdrawal.

acceptable (see Matthew 19:1-9). It would also include couples who are living together (or involved in a sexual relationship) but are not married, and all homosexual relationships.

Not only does Paul insist, in 1 Corinthians 5, that the church is to avoid keeping company with the sexually immoral, but he also includes a list of other sins that would be grounds for discipline. He wrote: "But now I have written to you not to keep company with anyone named a brother, who is a fornicator, or covetous, or an idolater, or a reviler, or a drunkard, or an extortioner—not even to eat with such as person" (5:11). This list is fairly self-explanatory. Any brother or sister who is known to be involved in any one of these sins should be disciplined. Almost as a side note, it would be interesting to know if any congregation in the United States of American in the last 30 years has withdrawn from any member due to covetousness. This writer can say he has never heard of such and would be amazed to hear that it has actually happened. If it has, the case would be so rare as to be negligible. Does that mean that we have had so few covetous brethren in the church for the past 30 years that no need existed to disfellowship them? Or would a better explanation be that the church as a whole has been so negligent to the New Testament's teaching on church discipline that we have almost lost the ability to recognize covetousness, much less judge correctly enough to withdraw from a brother or sister on the grounds of this sin in his or her life?

Another important aspect of church discipline can be observed in Paul's list of sins that would necessitate the practice. A fornicator is not a person who commits a one time act of fornication and is sorry and repents of that action. Nor is a drunkard a teenager who drinks at a party, decides it is not a godly thing to do, and avoids such action in the future. Just as a husband's working one day on the leaky faucet in his house does not make him a plumber, sins of fornication or drunkenness that happen in isolated instances would not classify someone under Paul's list as a fornicator or drunkard. Paul's list describes individuals whose habitual practices included covetousness, drunkenness, idolatry, and the like. It is a part of their lifestyle that is known to the congregation. This aspect of their lives they have refused to change, and continue to practice regardless of the encouragement they have received from their Christian family to repent. Furthermore, it should be obvious that Paul was not giving a comprehensive list of sins that would be grounds for discipline. Instead, he is trying to press the point that, not only is sexual sin grounds for withdrawal, but any habitual, sinful practice by someone called a brother would be grounds for church discipline.

> Any habitual, sinful practice by someone called a brother would be grounds for church discipline.

Various Other Sins

Other sins are listed in the New Testament as grounds for disfellowship. In writing to the Thessalonians in his second epistle, Paul forcefully condemns Christians in that church who had become lazy and refused to work. Paul commands the church to "withdraw from every brother who walks disorderly and not according to the tradition which he received from us" (2 Thessalonians 3:6). In his explanation of the "tradition" which he presented to them, Paul stresses the fact that he, as an apostle, worked with his own hands so that he would not burden the Christians there. He then noted that if a man was unwilling to work, he should not eat (3:6). Furthermore, he brought to light the fact that some of the Thessalonians had conducted themselves in a "disorderly manner" by refusing to work and becoming busybodies. Regarding such disorderly, non-working, busybodies, Paul commanded: "And if anyone does not obey our word in this epistle, note that person and do not keep company with him, that he may be ashamed. Yet do not count him as an enemy, but admonish him as a brother" (3:14-15).

> "Yet do not count him as an enemy, but admonish him as a brother."

In this specific context, the sins of idleness, laziness, refusal to work, and being a busybody are immediately under discussion. In our modern day, this would include those who are healthly and could get a job, but refuse to work, mooching off the church, their parents, spouses, or the government for their livelihood.

In addition to the specific sins listed by Paul, an underlying principle for determining grounds for church discipline becomes apparent to the reader. The "disorderly" Christians had not only refused to follow the example that Paul had shown them by working with his own hands, but it seems that they had persisted in their slothful ways in spite of continued instruction and edification. These Christians were stubbornly clinging to a lifestyle that had been clearly and repeatedly condemned by God's inspired apostle. The principle, then, that comes to light is that stubborn refusal to follow any of God's commands in the face of repeated admonition and warning would be grounds for disfellowship. It is also interesting to note that in 2 Thessalonians, as in 1 Corinthians, the grounds for withdrawal included a sinful habitual lifestyle. The disorderly Thessalonians had not committed a single, one-time act of which they had repented. They were involved in an ongoing, public lifestyle that could easily be witnessed by their fellow Christians.

Paul's instructions to Titus offer more insight into the attitudes and actions that would be grounds for withdrawal. He told Titus to "reject a divisive man…" (Titus 3:10-11). A divisive attitude provided grounds for withdrawal. Any person in a congregation who pits members against the leadership or against other members in an attempt to get his way would be considered divisive. Those who hold to an incorrect, unscriptural teaching but insist on their position being heard at every opportunity would fall into this category. A preacher who "rides a hobby horse," neglecting to teach the whole counsel of God, constantly preaching against a certain "faction" in the congregation who might hold a different opinion than he holds on a non-doctrinal issue would be considered divisive.

Embedded in Paul's instructions to Titus is another useful principle for determining grounds for withdrawal. The divisive man was to be given two warnings or admonitions before he was rejected. This would indicate that the church's discipline was not a knee-jerk reaction done without consideration on the part of congregation. Rather it consisted of earnest planning and pleading on the part of the young preacher and the church. Here again, as in the other instances, the divisive man maintained a sinful attitude and lifestyle that he refused to alter. He was a habitually divisive individual who refused to respond to loving correction.

Additionally, the apostle John's instructions to the "elect lady" in 2 John supply another important aspect to the discussion. John wrote: "If anyone comes to you and does not bring this doctrine, do not receive him into your house nor greet him for he who greets him shares in his evil deeds" (10-11). Admittedly, many aspects of these instructions lie outside the scope of this discussion. But the important point to be stressed is that improper teaching and the spreading of false doctrine would be grounds for rejection or withdrawal. For example, a Christian who teaches others that baptism is not essential for salvation would be a candidate for rejection or withdrawal. Those who would hold and propagate unscriptural notions concerning marriage, divorce, and remarriage would also fall into this category, as well as those who might teach unbiblical tenants regarding the resurrection, the deity of Christ, or the inspiration of the Bible. Unscriptural teaching can be grounds for disfellowship.

> **Improper teaching and the spreading of false doctrine would be grounds for rejection or withdrawal.**

CONCLUSION

The inspired New Testament writers enumerate several specific sins that would provide grounds for withdrawal, such as sexual immorality, covetousness, idolatry, sinful idleness, divisiveness, and false teaching. Fundamental principles are also given by which all other sinful actions and lifestyles should be considered. Any Christian who persists in a rebellious, sinful lifestyle in spite of proper instruction, after being admonished and lovingly warned to repent, should be disciplined. As with many aspects of the internal workings of a congregation, deciding if a brother's or sister's lifestyle elicits withdrawal is a decision that should be approached humbly, prayerfully, and carefully with the determination to do what is spiritually best for the individual brother or sister as well as for the congregation.

Chapter 12

Discussion questions

1. What is meant by a "habitual lifestyle?" What is an impenitent heart? How do these two ideas relate to church discipline?

2. List and discuss several specific sins listed in the Bible that call for disciplinary action. Include passages such as 1 Corinthians 5:10-11 and 2 Thessalonians 3:6ff in your answer.

3. Explain why some sins would not call for public discipline. Examine the attitudes that contrast sins that would call for discipline and those that would not.

4. What is probably the most obvious sin that would elicit disfellowship? How has this sin crept into our congregations? Why has this sin had such an infiltrating effect?

5. Why are certain sins difficult to pinpoint and identify? What steps could be taken to more accurately diagnose these sins? How would passages like Hebrews 5:12-14 and Philippians 1:9 factor into this discussion?

Chapter 13

A Biblical Test Case

One can only imagine the spiritual progress and impact that congregations could make if they would "purge out the old leaven" and separate themselves from the spiritually crippling effects of sin.

Chapter 13

"Therefore I rejoice that I have confidence in you in everything."
(2 Corinthians 7:16)

One would be hard pressed to find a more fitting conclusion to any study on church discipline than an analysis of the procedure as it was implemented by the Corinthian church at the instigation of the inspired apostle Paul. The Corinthian church's response to Paul's instructions, as well as the effect their obedience had on the wayward brother, truly are some of the most encouraging, uplifting examples in Scripture.

Sinful Brother Identified

One of the interesting aspects of the disciplinary action in the Corinthian church is that the sinful brother's lifestyle was well known to the entire congregation. Even Paul had heard of the sexual immorality committed by this brother. He further understood that the Corinthians not only allowed this wayward brother to stay in their fellowship, but somehow found reason to boast about their tolerance (1 Corinthians 5:1-2a).

Lack of Discipline Rebuked

Paul quickly brought to the attention of the Corinthian church that their boasting was entirely misplaced. Instead, they should have withdrawn fellowship from the wayward brother in an attempt to save his soul. He sharply rebuked them for their failure to do so (1 Corinthians 5:2-3).

Discipline Commanded

Upon rebuking the Corinthians for their lack of action in regard to the sinful brother, Paul commanded them to withdraw fellowship from him. In order to add the proper weight to the command that it deserved, he informed the church that they should withdraw from this brother "in the name of our Lord Jesus Christ…along with my spirit, with the power of our Lord Jesus Christ" (1 Corinthians 5:4).

Rationale Given for Withdrawal

After issuing a direct command from God to disfellowship this sinful brother, Paul offers two primary reasons for undertaking such a drastic endeavor. First, the process was an attempt to save the spirit of the wayward brother "in the day of the Lord Jesus." Second, the process was designed to purge the church of the sinful influence of such a person, and help prevent other Christians in the church from following such a sinful example (1 Corinthians 5:5-7).

ADDITIONAL SINS ENUMERATED THAT WOULD MERIT WITHDRAWAL

Once the rationale for withdrawal was offered, Paul listed other sins that would elicit disfellowship. Understanding that such a procedure might need to be administered in the future, the apostle enumerated specific sins and guiding principles by which the congregation could proceed in any future cases that would require withdrawal (1 Corinthians 5:9-13).

THE CORINTHIAN CHURCH OBEYS PAUL'S COMMANDS

Paul's stinging rebuke and emphatic command to withdraw from the sinful brother did not fall on deaf ears. The penitent Corinthians exhibited an attitude of contrite obedience and implemented the disciplinary procedures (2 Corinthians 2:3-6).

The Wayward Brother Returns

The obedient actions of the Corinthian church had the desired effect. Upon feeling the force of the loss of fellowship with his spiritual family, the wayward brother repented and desired earnestly to be allowed back into the congregation's fellowship (2 Corinthians 2:6-8).

Paul Urges Forgiveness

So determined were the Corinthians to obey God's command to withdraw from the sinful brother, it seems they needed additional encouragement to reaffirm their love for him. Their withdrawal had accomplished its goal, the sinful brother repented, and it was time to accept him back into fellowship. A spirit of forgiveness and acceptance was to pervade their relationship with this penitent brother.

Wrapping Up the Process

Although we do not have any insight into the

Corinthians' reaction to Paul's instruction to forgive the sinful brother, it would seem a fair assumption, based on their obedience to withdraw from him, to conclude that they obeyed Paul and welcomed the brother back into the fold.

Oh, that our 21st century congregations would have such a spirit that they would prayerfully consider the powerful example provided by the Corinthians in regard to church discipline. It is the obligation of every Christian and congregation to re-examine our failure of this test of obedience, be willing to repent like the Corinthians did, and begin separating ourselves from sin. One can only imagine the spiritual progress and impact that congregations could make if they would "purge out the old leaven" and separate themselves from the spiritually crippling effects of sin. How wonderful it would be if Paul could say to our present day congregations what he said to the Corinthians upon their obedience to his commands: "Therefore I rejoice that I have confidence in you in everything" (2 Corinthians 7:16).

Chapter 13
Discussion questions

1. What is the ultimate desired effect of church discipline? Name some other purposes for the procedure.

2. If church discipline is done in a loving, obedient way, what type of responsibility does a congregation have in regard to the ultimate outcome of the process?

3. Discuss the idea of "purging out old leaven." What are some biblical illustrations of this idea? What is the purpose? How do you think God's attitude toward sin factors into disfellowship?

4. What was the outcome of Paul's teaching the Corinthian brethren about discipline? What steps did the Corinthians take in response to Paul's instructions? How did those steps affect the sinful brother? How did they affect the congregation?

5. What attitude should a congregation adopt toward the penitent brother or sister who is disciplined? What might occur if the proper attitude is not adopted in regard to the congregation as well as the one who is disciplined?

Appendix A

Self Withdrawal

Can Members "Withdraw" Themselves?

When a wayward brother or sister is faced with the prospect of public discipline, it is common for him or her to try to avoid being exposed publicly. One of the most frequent tactics to avoid public exposure is for the wayward Christian to "withdraw" himself from the congregation. Since he has withdrawn himself, he reasons, he is no longer a member of the congregation, and, thus, they have no right to openly expose his sin. It often is the case that the elders or men of a congregation who are considering public withdrawal of a wayward Christian are stumped by this maneuver. In many instances, the leaders of the congregation do not really want to follow through with the public withdrawal mandated in the Bible, and this "self-removal" seems to offer them a way to avoid the painful process. Can a Christian "withdraw" himself from a congregation to avoid being publicly disciplined?

Once a Christian, Always a Christian

One very important aspect of the Christian life is the fact that once people become Christians, the

Appendix A — Self Withdrawal

Bible considers those people to be different from the world. It is not the case that once Christians are saved, they are always saved. But it is the case that their status forever changes when they become Christians. For instance, in Acts 8, Simon the sorcerer believed in Christ, was baptized, and was added to the Church by the Lord (Acts 8:13; 2:47). But soon after his baptized, he attempted to buy the miraculous power of the Holy Spirit. Peter vehemently rebuked his worldly thinking. He said to Simon, "Your money perish with you" (Acts 8:20). His statement implied that Simon was in a lost condition soon after his baptism. Peter then explained to Simon what he needed to do to get right with the Lord. Peter told him to repent of his wickedness and pray to God for forgiveness. Notice that Simon did not have to get baptized again. He was told simply to repent and pray. No non-Christians were ever told to repent and pray for their salvation or forgiveness. Even though Simon was apparently in a lost condition soon after his baptism, his status was that of a wayward Christian, not that of a person in the world.

Examples of wayward Christians are numerous. In Revelation 3, Jesus sent word to the Laodiceans that they were luke warm. Because of their tepid spiritual status, Jesus explained that He would spit them out of His mouth, or vomit them away from His presence. It is interesting to note, however, that He addresses the church with the same introductory greeting as He does the faithful church of Philadelphia. The Laodiceans were Christians, but they were erring Christians.

The apostle Paul provided an even more specific example of this "wayward-Christian status" in 2 Thessalonians 3:14-15. Immediately after Paul commanded the Thessalonians to avoid keeping company with the disorderly brother or sister in their midst, he stated, "Yet do not count him as an enemy, but admonish him as a brother." Even when a Christian is properly withdrawn from, that person is still admonished "as a brother." Following that line of reasoning then, suppose that a Christian "withdraws" himself from a congregation. Is that brother no longer a Christian? He certainly is a Christian and should still be treated as "a brother"–but an erring one.

We can glean further insight into this matter from Paul's statements to the Corinthians. In 1 Corinthians 5, following his forceful demands that the Corinthians remove the sexually immoral brother from their midst, Paul said: "I wrote to you in my epistle not to keep company with sexually immoral people. Yet I certainly did not mean with the sexually immoral people of this world…since then you would need to go out of the world. But now I have written to you not to keep company with anyone named a brother who is a fornicator…not even to eat with such a person" (5:10-11). Consider Paul's statements carefully. The Corinthians were commanded to avoid eating with anyone called "a brother" who was practicing a sinful life style. But we have seen that when a Christian is withdrawn from, that person continues to be a brother in Christ, albeit an erring one. Would it be the case that the Corinthians must avoiding eating with a brother from whom the elders withdrew, but could continue eating with a brother who "withdrew" himself? Certainly not. The Bible leaves no loophole for a wayward Christian to avoid public church discipline by withdrawing himself or herself prior to the public proceedings regarding the withdrawal process.

"Recognizing" a Christian's Self Withdrawal

It is true that once lost sinners become Christians, they are always considered brothers or sisters, even though they might be wayward and lost. But it is also true that fellowship with the Lord's church is a personal choice. The Lord's army has always been composed of volunteers. And the Lord allows Christians to decide, on a daily basis, whether they want to remain in the fellowship of His family, the church. In 1 John 4:7, we are told that the requisite to remain in fellowship with the Lord and His Church is to walk in the light, or have a habitual practice of obedience to God's commands. If a person desires to break his fellowship with the Lord and the church, he can do so at any time. Yet his self withdrawal does not exempt him from public discipline.

Practically speaking, a Christian's "self withdrawal" hardly, if at all, alters a congregation's actions toward the brother. Suppose a brother understands that the church is about to disfellowship him. In an attempt to avoid being publicly disciplined, he declares that he is severing his fellowship with the

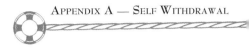

congregation. What should be done? The elders or leaders of the congregation should simply continue the procedure and announce the man's sins publicly as planned. They could then explain that the wayward brother has stated that he is no longer in fellowship with the Lord's church, and that the congregation recognizes this brother's status as an erring brother no longer in fellowship with the saints. It is ironic that a person who "withdraws" himself is basically saying that he recognizes he is no longer in fellowship with the Lord's Church, which is exactly the status that is already recognized by the Lord and the church. The erring brother should be publicly noted and avoided, but admonished as a brother in accordance with Paul's commands in 2 Thessalonians 3:14-15. It is impossible for Christians to so remove themselves that the church should not longer admonish them as erring brethren.

Appendix B

An Actual Letter Sent By An Elder To His Daughter On Behalf Of The Congregation And Eldership

[NOTE: The following is an actual letter sent by an elder to his daughter on behalf of the congregation and eldership. Minor changes have been made to keep the parties anonymous and to help the letter fit into book format. The deep, personal sentiments portrayed in the letter embody the spirit and magnitude of church discipline.]

Dear Daughter,

This may be one of the most awkward letters I have ever written. It is very personal in the sense that it is a father writing to a daughter. It is also personal in that it is a reflection and expression of many who have come to know you personally. This is the final plea of a father and mother, an eldership, and a congregation for you to please come home. It is not the end of the congregation encouraging you to come home; but it is the last correspondence this eldership will send before we announce before the congregation your deliberate refusal to return.

It is difficult to understand why anyone would have to plead so for your return based upon your own words. You have expressed yourself how everyone here at the congregation treated you with genuine courtesy and respect. You also have told us many times how much peace you had by just being with the people here and how you need this interaction with such people. We would assume that you have little doubt as to the concern everyone has for you by the cards and phone calls you received. Even though you did not answer nor return your phone calls, you still must be impressed with the desire of others to talk with you. You have also stated the horror you have of passing from this life in your present condition. All of these will be forgotten in time as the heart grows more distant and the conscience more calloused (Heb.3:8, 13, 15; 4:7; 1 Tim. 4:2).

On a very personal level I beg you as a father to return and begin a climb that I realize will be difficult but far, far from impossible. The Lord Himself realized it would be a straight, hard way at its best (Mat. 7:13). You also know that very few people have life at its best. All have their struggles. Some of the best memories of my life are those that include you. We talked together, prayed together, visited/campaigned together and some times just played. To me you will always be "daddy's little girl," you know that. As for Sally, regardless of how much she is taught and knows, there is no one to her like her mother. Even though she is not with you, you will have more impact upon her life as to what she becomes than all of us put together. Will she survive the challenge to be faithful? Will she make the choices that will ensure her a happy home life in her future? And what hope will Sally have? To a great degree the answers to those questions rest with you.

The choice is yours. If you chose not to return, your decision will be made known to the congregation on _____. This will change our relationship as well as your relationship with the members at the congregation until you do what you know very well is the right thing to do (2 Thess. 3:6, 14, 15). Take the time and read (Luke 15:11-24). Maybe this will help. We love you.

Elders